Pray, Praise & Give Thanks

Jesus Teaches Us to Pray

Cross Explorations

Growing in Christ

Level B
Teacher Guide

CONCORDIA PUBLISHING HOUSE · SAINT LOUIS

3558 S. Jefferson Ave., St. Louis, MO 63118-3968
1-800-325-3040 • www.cph.org

Written by Diane Grebing

Edited by Brenda Trunkhill

Manufactured in the United States of America

Growing in Christ® is published by Concordia Publishing House. Your comments and suggestions concerning this material are appreciated. Email us at sundayschool@cph.org.

Contents

Introduction		4
Lesson 1	Daniel in the Lions' Den	13
Lesson 2	Jesus Heals the Centurion's Servant	21
Lesson 3	Peter and John Heal a Lame Man	29
Lesson 4	Jesus Teaches His Disciples to Pray	37
Lesson 5	The Baptism of Jesus	45
Lesson 6	Zacchaeus	53
Lesson 7	Paul and Silas in Prison	61
Lesson 8	Job	69
Lesson 9	God Provides Manna and Quail	77
Lesson 10	Joseph Forgives His Brothers	85
Lesson 11	The Temptation of Jesus	93
Lesson 12	Three Men in a Fiery Furnace	101
Lesson 13	The Saints in Heaven	109
Teacher Resource Pages		117

God Listens to You

In *Pray, Praise & Give Thanks: Jesus Teaches Us to Pray*, students search thirteen Bible stories to learn about the Lord's Prayer. They will see how these petitions taught by Jesus are meaningful for them.

Pray, Praise & Give Thanks: Jesus Teaches Us to Pray offers two levels. Level B (this guide) is designed for students who are independent readers; in most cases, this means students who have finished grades 2–6. Level A is for children who are nonreaders—generally preschool through those who have finished grade 1.

Features of the Teacher Guide

- Easy-to-use four-step lesson plans for each week
- Suggestions for snacks and worship
- Reproducible student activity pages for each lesson
- Age-appropriate ways to teach the Bible story and apply it to young lives
- A Bible study for the teacher, titled "Preparing the Lesson"
- "Living the Faith" suggestions for extending the lesson truths beyond the classroom
- Perforated pages to make team teaching or small-group/large-group teaching easier
- Helpful CD icon on pages that are also found on the Director CD

Teacher Tip

You will want to decorate your classroom. Decorate the area where your students arrive to look like a ticket booth. Create a Ferris wheel with pockets to hold tickets for each child near your classroom altar. If you designate a Bible storytelling area, you could decorate it as an arena called "Blue-Ribbon Bible Stories." If your congregation is using CPH's *Barnyard Roundup* VBS, you may wish to use some of the VBS decorating materials to help decorate your Sunday School area as well.

What You Will Need

- This Teacher Guide
- Items listed on the Materials list in each lesson
- Bibles, catechisms, hymnal, children's songbook, and an offering basket
- Scissors, tape, glue, paper, crayons or markers, pencils, and other standard classroom supplies
- *All God's People Sing!* (*AGPS*) and *Lutheran Service Book* (*LSB*) (from CPH)

The Four-Step Lesson Plan

Opening

- Introduces the lesson theme and activates prior knowledge to prepare students for the lesson. As a help, invite an adult volunteer to prepare and teach this activity for you each week.
- Provides an Opening ritual; suggestions for large-group openings are found on the Director CD

God Speaks

- Teaches the Bible story and reviews the details using the student leaflet as an aid in investigating the lesson
- Teaches the Bible Words

We Live

- Applies the Law and Gospel in the text to the students' lives
- Provides a craft option to help students learn the key point
- Offers multiple activities to choose what works best with your class

Closing

- Provides a closing song and prayer
- Gives suggestions to help students apply what they learned beyond the classroom

Student Leaflets

There are colorful, four-page leaflets, available as a separate purchase, to go with each lesson in this curriculum. The leaflets have the Bible story, a Bible-story hidden picture, review activities, and a prayer. They make a great take-home piece for family use.

Director CD

This CD, available for purchase, has many additional resources:

- Reproducible Opening outline
- Opening devotions
- Bible Words
- Snack ideas
- Craft ideas
- "Preparing the Lesson" Bible studies
- Decorating ideas
- Reproducible pages
- Clip art
- Bulletin notes
- Hymn and song recordings

Pray, Praise & Give Thanks
Jesus Teaches Us to Pray

	Take-Home Point	Bible Words	Catechism Connection	Welcome & Opening (about 15 minutes)
1  **Daniel in the Lions' Den** Daniel 6:1–27	God hears my prayers.	In the day of my trouble I call upon You, for You answer me. Psalm 86:7	Prayer is speaking to God in words and thoughts. (Question 194) We should pray to the true God only, Father, Son, and Holy Spirit, not to idols, saints, or anything God has created. (Question 195)	**"Fair"ly Good Clue** Microphone **Worship** Prayer at the Fair Devotion: A Scary Moment
2  **Jesus Heals the Centurion's Servant** Matthew 8:5–13	God tells me to pray for everything.	I urge that supplications, prayers, intercessions, and thanksgivings be made for all people. 1 Timothy 2:1	We should ask for everything that tends to the glory of God and to our own and our neighbor's welfare, both spiritual and bodily blessings. (Question 197)	**"Fair"ly Good Clue** Red Cross symbol **Worship** Prayer at the Fair Devotion: Answered Prayers
3  **Peter and John Heal a Lame Man** Acts 3:1–10	God is worthy of my thanks and praise.	Give thanks to the Lord, for He is good, for His steadfast love endures forever. Psalm 136:1	We should also praise and thank God for who He is and what He has done. (Question 197)	**"Fair"ly Good Clue** Blue ribbon **Worship** Prayer at the Fair Devotion: In the Show-Ring
4  **Jesus Teaches His Disciples to Pray** Luke 11:1–13	Jesus teaches me how to pray.	Ask, and it will be given to you; seek, and you will find; knock, and it will be opened to you. Matthew 7:7	Jesus gave us the Lord's Prayer [to show us how to pray]. (Question 204)	**"Fair"ly Good Clue** Signboard **Worship** Prayer at the Fair Devotion: A Special Demonstration

Bible Story & Leaflet Review (about 20 minutes)	Bible Application (about 5 minutes)	Craft (about 10 minutes)	Snack (about 5 minutes)	Closing (about 5 minutes)
Learn that Daniel called upon the one true God, who heard Daniel's prayer and protected him in the lions' den. God hears our prayers and protects us from sin, death, and the devil.	*Do a crossword puzzle to remind us that prayer is how we communicate with God.*	*Prayer Wheel Passenger Pockets*	*Popping Corn*	Review the lesson truth. Sing songs and pray. Send information home to families.
Learn that the centurion prayed for his servant to be healed. God invites us to pray for our needs and the needs of others.	*Talk about interceding for others in specific situations.*	*Prayer Reminder Wreath*	*Food on a Stick*	
Learn that the lame man praised and thanked God. We pray, praise, and give thanks to God for who He is and what He has done for us through His Son, Jesus.	*Look up Bible passages that describe characteristics of our blue-ribbon God.*	*Our Blue-Ribbon God*	*Blue-Ribbon Cake*	
Learn that Jesus taught His disciples and followers the Lord's Prayer to show them how to pray. God invites us to talk to Him using this same prayer today.	*Highlight the sections of the Lord's Prayer.*	*The Lord's Prayer Plaques*	*Prayer Pretzels*	

Pray, Praise & Give Thanks
Jesus Teaches Us to Pray

Lesson	Take-Home Point	Bible Words	Catechism Connection	Welcome & Opening (about 15 minutes)
5  **The Baptism of Jesus** Luke 3:15–22	God wants me to pray to Him.	See what kind of love the Father has given to us, that we should be called children of God. 1 John 3:1	The word *Father* tells us that God loves us and wants us to pray to Him confidently and without fear. (Question 205)	**"Fair"ly Good Clue** Cell phone **Worship** Prayer at the Fair Devotion: Time with Dad
6  **Zacchaeus** Luke 19:1–10	God helps me keep His name holy.	Let your light shine before others, so that they may see your good works and give glory to your Father who is in heaven. Matthew 5:16	We keep God's name holy when God's Word is taught among us in its truth and purity [and] when we live according to the Word of God. (Question 210)	**"Fair"ly Good Clue** Entry form **Worship** Prayer at the Fair Devotion: Giving God Glory
7  **Paul and Silas in Prison** Acts 16:16–34	God works through me to make His kingdom grow.	The kingdom of God is at hand; repent and believe in the gospel. Mark 1:15	We ask God to give us His Holy Spirit so that we believe His Word and lead godly lives as members of His kingdom of grace; bring many others into His kingdom of grace; [and] use us to extend His kingdom of grace. (Question 213)	**"Fair"ly Good Clue** Basket of corn **Worship** Prayer at the Fair Devotion: An Invitation
8  **Job** Job 1:1–2:10; 42	God keeps me strong in faith.	For I know that my Redeemer lives. Job 19:25	God's will is done when He breaks . . . the plans of the devil, the world, and our sinful nature, which try to destroy our faith . . . [and when He] keeps us firm in His Word and faith and helps us lead God-pleasing lives. (Question 218)	**"Fair"ly Good Clue** Barbells **Worship** Prayer at the Fair Devotion: Staying Strong
9  **God Provides Manna and Quail** Exodus 16	God gives me what I need.	The eyes of all look to You, and You give them their food in due season. You open Your hand; You satisfy the desire of every living thing. Psalm 145:15–16	We pray to God for daily bread . . . because Christ wants us to realize that our entire life . . . depends on God [and] look to God for physical as well as spiritual blessings. (Question 219)	**"Fair"ly Good Clue** Jar of home-canned pickles **Worship** Prayer at the Fair Devotion: God's Bountiful Blessings

Bible Story & Leaflet Review (about 20 minutes)	Bible Application (about 5 minutes)	Craft (about 10 minutes)	Snack (about 5 minutes)	Closing (about 5 minutes)
Learn that God, our Father in heaven, who has made us His children through water and the Word, invites us to come to Him without fear.	*Crack the coded words to find out about our relationship with our heavenly Father.*	*Child of God "Selfie" Props*	*Snow Cones*	Review the lesson truth. Sing songs and pray. Send information home to families.
Learn that Zacchaeus joyfully responded to His Savior's invitation, showing the Word of God at work in him. We keep God's name holy and glorify God as we live according to His Word, letting His light shine.	*Look at situations in which people are hallowing God's name.*	*Glorifying God Quilt*	*Glory Cakes*	
Learn that through the witness of Paul and Silas to the Philippian jailer and his family, the kingdom of God grew. We ask that God help us live according to His Word and use us to extend His kingdom of grace.	*See situations in which the Holy Spirit is making the kingdom grow.*	*Witness Bracelets*	*Corny Treats*	
Learn that despite Job's troubles, God is faithful and did not allow the devil to destroy Job's faith. Amidst our troubles, God strengthens us through His Word and keeps us in faith to life everlasting.	*Read Bible verses to learn about God's strength.*	*God Gives Strength Barbells*	*Power Mix*	
Learn that God provided for the children of Israel. We can trust God to provide all that we need.	*Search and find 15 examples of "daily bread."*	*Daily Bread Jar*	*Jars of Goodness*	

Pray, Praise & Give Thanks
Jesus Teaches Us to Pray

Lesson	Take-Home Point	Bible Words	Catechism Connection	Welcome & Opening (about 15 minutes)
10  **Joseph Forgives His Brothers** Genesis 37:12–36; 45:1–15; 50:15–21	God forgives me and wants me to forgive others.	Be kind . . . forgiving one another, as God in Christ forgave you. Ephesians 4:32	We ask that our Father in heaven would for Christ's sake graciously forgive our sins. (Question 224) Our heavenly Father wants us to forgive and to do good to those who sin against us. (Question 226)	**"Fair"ly Good Clue** Milk bottle carnival game **Worship** Prayer at the Fair Devotion: A Lesson in Forgiveness
11  **The Temptation of Jesus** Matthew 4:1–11	God helps me resist temptation.	Be watchful. Your adversary the devil prowls around like a roaring lion. . . . Resist him, firm in your faith. 1 Peter 5:8–9	The devil, the world, and our sinful nature try to mislead us into false belief, despair, and other great sins. (Question 229) We ask our Father in heaven to give us strength to resist and overcome temptations. (Question 230)	**"Fair"ly Good Clue** Tractor pull **Worship** Prayer at the Fair Devotion: Tempted Tummies
12  **Three Men in a Fiery Furnace** Daniel 3	God rescues me from every evil.	The Lord will rescue me from every evil deed and bring me safely into His heavenly kingdom. 2 Timothy 4:18	The Lord keeps us from harm and helps us to endure the troubles that He allows to come into our lives. (Question 232) We want [God] to keep us faithful to Him and when we die to take us . . . to Himself in heaven. (Question 233)	**"Fair"ly Good Clue** Ring-of-fire motorcycle stunt **Worship** Prayer at the Fair Devotion: Delivered from Danger
13  **The Saints in Heaven** Revelation 19:1–10	God has power to answer my prayers.	Salvation and glory and power belong to our God. Revelation 19:1	*Amen* means "so shall it be" and emphasizes that God . . . will hear our prayers and answer them. (Question 234) [God] alone is the King who has all good gifts in His control. He alone has the power to grant our petitions. He has all glory and is worthy of our praise. (Question 235)	**"Fair"ly Good Clue** Fireworks **Worship** Prayer at the Fair Devotion: Explosions of Praise

Bible Story & Leaflet Review (about 20 minutes)	Bible Application (about 5 minutes)	Craft (about 10 minutes)	Snack (about 5 minutes)	Closing (about 5 minutes)
Learn that despite their sins against him, Joseph forgave his brothers. Despite our sins, God forgives us for Jesus' sake and helps us to forgive others.	*See how to knock down sins, burdens, and hurts.*	*Dry-Erase Memo Boards*	*Homemade Lemonade*	Review the lesson truth. Sing songs and pray. Send information home to families.
Learn that Jesus resisted the temptations of the devil and kept God's Law for us because we cannot. Jesus strengthens us through His Word to resist temptation and assures us that He has won the victory over sin, death, and the devil for us.	*Look up Bible verses to learn about standing strong against temptation's pull.*	*Temptation Shields*	*Corn Dogs*	
Learn that God rescued the three faithful young men from the fiery furnace. God rescues us from harm and helps us endure the troubles that He allows to come into our lives.	*Choose encouraging Bible verses for each person facing evil.*	*God Rescues Us Cup Activity*	*Nachos, Cheese, and Salsa*	
Learn that the saints in heaven praise God for His power and glory and wisdom. God, who is all powerful, loving, and wise, will answer our prayers as He has promised.	*Do a Bible study to see the power behind our prayers.*	*Hallelujah Banner*	*Cotton Candy*	

A Responsive Reading on Prayer

(based on *Luther's Small Catechism with Explanation*, Questions 193–203)

Leader: God commands and invites believers in Jesus Christ to pray.

Students: **Rejoice always, pray without ceasing, give thanks in all circumstances; for this is the will of God in Christ Jesus for you.** (1 Thessalonians 5:16–18)

Leader: Prayer is speaking to God in words and thoughts.

Students: **Let the words of my mouth and the meditation of my heart be acceptable in Your sight, O Lord, my rock and my redeemer.** (Psalm 19:14)

Leader: We pray only to the true God, Father, Son, and Holy Spirit. In our prayers we should ask for everything that gives glory to God and that would be for our own and our neighbor's good, including both spiritual and bodily blessings. We should also praise and thank God for who He is and what He has done.

Students: **Do not be anxious about anything, but in everything by prayer and supplication with thanksgiving let your requests be made known to God.** (Philippians 4:6)

Leader: We should pray in Jesus' name, with confidence, and according to God's will.

Students: **This is the confidence that we have toward [God], that if we ask anything according to His will He hears us.** (1 John 5:14)

Leader: God hears the prayers of all Christians and answers in His own way and at His own time.

Students: **Before they call I will answer; while they are yet speaking I will hear.** (Isaiah 65:24)

Leader: We should pray for ourselves and for all other people, even our enemies. We should pray everywhere. We should pray regularly and frequently, especially in time of trouble.

Students: **[God says,] "Call upon Me in the day of trouble; I will deliver you, and you shall glorify Me."** (Psalm 50:15)

Lesson 1

Preparing the Lesson

Daniel in the Lions' Den

Daniel 6:1–27—God hears my prayers.

Key Point

Daniel called upon the one true God, who heard Daniel's prayer and protected him in the lions' den. God hears our prayers and protects us from sin, death, and the devil.

Law/**Gospel**

This sinful world, Satan, and my own sinful flesh all conspire against me to turn me away from faith in God. The commandments stand firm: you shall have no other gods; you shall not misuse the name of the Lord your God. **The triune God is the only true God. He forgives my sins for Jesus' sake, gives me faith and strengthens it through His Word and Sacraments, and promises to hear my prayers and give me what I need.**

Context

Babylon, under the reign of King Nebuchadnezzar, conquered Judah and led away captives. Daniel and many of the smartest and wealthiest people were among the captives. Daniel was chosen to serve in the court of King Nebuchadnezzar and, under God's blessing, proved himself to be a wise counselor to the king, even rising above the king's Babylonian advisors. This created jealousy against Daniel. In this foreign country of Babylon, people did not worship the one true God. Even in the midst of false worship and persecution, Daniel remained faithful to the true God and continued to pray and worship Him alone.

Commentary

The account of Daniel's life is ripe with imagery. Daniel is a Christ figure. The satraps are satanic figures, setting Daniel up to be accused of crimes. The lions' den can be compared to hell and eternal damnation. When the satraps succeed in sentencing Daniel to death by throwing him into the lions' den, he overcomes it by the power of God and rises out of the pit. His accusers in turn are cast into "hell" and are destroyed (Psalm 9:15). This is a picture of Christ's suffering, death, and resurrection.

Daniel's fellow high officials were jealous of his gifts of leadership and wisdom. They couldn't find any fault in him, so they devised a way to trap him on account of his faith. If someone wanted to find fault with us, it wouldn't be terribly difficult. We tend to our needs at the cost of others. We too often speak poorly about other people. We are lazy in our work and school duties. We neglect God's Word and prayer even after His command to pray and His promise to hear. But Daniel's enemies could find no fault with his life or work.

So they set a trap for Daniel. They manipulated the king to create a law forbidding prayer to anyone but the king for thirty days. Daniel, however, remained faithful to God's Word. He never ceased to pray, refusing to follow the king's new law even for just thirty days. He didn't sneak off and do it privately in a hidden spot. Instead, he prayed openly three times a day, kneeling and facing Jerusalem in front of open windows. And he didn't just "pray in his heart or mind." He prayed with his voice and body.

Daniel broke the law by remaining faithful to God, and the satraps accused him before King Darius. They also accused the king of not wanting to enforce his law. They reminded him that his law, like all laws of the Medes and Persians, could not be ignored, broken, or changed.

The king must command that Daniel be punished as the law demands, and so he did. But he also pleaded with Daniel to pray to God for deliverance. Then he went back and fasted that night on Daniel's behalf.

The living God, who alone hears prayers, sent an angel to shut the lions' mouths. The law was fulfilled and the condemnation imposed, but miraculously, the innocent Daniel came forth from the lions' den the next day with no harm. God had saved him! Then, the king threw the accusers and their families into the lions' den, and they were destroyed. After that, the king made a new decree: all the people in his dominion were to tremble and fear before Daniel's God, the one living, eternal God, whose kingdom never ends, who delivers and rescues, who works signs and wonders in heaven and on earth.

So, too, God, who listened to Daniel's prayers and saved him from the power of the lions, saves us from sin, death, and that prowling lion, the devil, through His Son, Jesus. He invites us to call upon Him and promises to answer our prayers for Jesus' sake.

To hear an in-depth discussion of this Bible account, visit cph.org/podcast and listen to our Seeds of Faith podcast each week.

Lesson 1

Daniel in the Lions' Den

Daniel 6:1–27

Connections

Bible Words
In the day of my trouble I call upon You, for You answer me. Psalm 86:7

Faith Word
prayer

Hymns and Songs
The King's Kids Are Prayin' (Director CD 9)
I Am Trusting Thee, Lord Jesus (*LSB* 729)
Children of the Heavenly Father (*LSB* 725; Director CD 1)

Catechism
Prayer is speaking to God in words and thoughts. (Question 194)
We should pray to the true God only, Father, Son, and Holy Spirit, not to idols, saints, or anything God has created. (Question 195)

Take-Home Point
God hears my prayers.

1 Opening (15 minutes)

Welcome

To Prepare: Before class, decorate your classroom to look like a festive county fair. Set up a desk near the entrance of your classroom to be the ticket booth. Make a sign that says, "Welcome to the Christian County Fair." In one corner of the room, designate a worship area. Hang colorful plastic or paper triangular flags on which you've printed the words *Worship Place* or something similar, one letter per flag. Use the Ferris wheel pattern found on the Director CD to make and color a large poster-board wheel and hang it on a wall in the worship area. If you designate a Bible storytelling area, you could decorate it as an arena called "Blue-Ribbon Bible Stories." See the Director CD for more ideas. Make copies of the Lesson 1 fair ticket (Director CD) for each child.

Web Activity: Locate information about your area's county fair using the key words "[County name] County Fair." Preview all web activities before class.

Sit behind the ticket window and greet students as they arrive. Give each person a Lesson 1 ticket.

Say **Welcome to our Sunday School course, *Pray, Praise & Give Thanks: Jesus Teaches Us to Pray.* You've just come through the main gate of the Christian County Fair. Take a look at the ticket. Let's read out loud together what the ticket says at the top: "One Free Admission." Wow!**

Ask **How many of you have ever been to a fair?** (Let the students respond.) **What are some things you saw there** (or something you think might be there)**?** (Animals, rides, food stands, shows, concerts, exhibits)

MATERIALS NEEDED

1 Opening	2 God Speaks	3 We Live	4 Closing
Director CD Christian County Fair decorations (see Director CD) White poster board Lesson 1 fair tickets (printed from the Director CD) Copies of "A Responsive Reading on Prayer" (Director CD or p. 12) Resource Page 1 Microphone (does not have to work)	Student Leaflet 1 Bibles	Bibles Activity Page 1 6 × 9-inch white envelopes or small gift/favor boxes Poster-board Ferris wheel pattern (see Director CD) Masking tape Self-adhesive plastic gems Sparkly pipe cleaners	Director CD Lesson 1 fair tickets Microphone (does not have to work)

Say **Here at the Christian County Fair, each week you'll enter through this same gate and explore Bible stories that teach us about prayer and the special prayer Jesus taught us called the Lord's Prayer. Every week will have a special theme. Today's fair theme is found on your ticket: God hears my prayers. Let's head over to the worship area to begin our time at the fair with song and prayer.** Move to the worship area.

Worship

Sing "The King's Kids Are Prayin'" (Director CD 9) or "I Am Trusting Thee, Lord Jesus" (*LSB* 729). These songs emphasize that God hears our prayers.

Invocation **In the name of the Father and of the Son and of the Holy Spirit. Amen.**

Hand out copies of "A Responsive Reading on Prayer" (Director CD or p. 12).

Say **Every week we will use this reading to learn more about what it means to pray to our triune God.** Use the reading together.

A "Fair"ly Good Clue to Learn a Fact about Prayer

Bring out the microphone.

Ask **What is this object?** (A microphone) **For what is a microphone used?** (A microphone amplifies a voice so it can be heard.)

Say **Take out your ticket. Look for the microphone. This is a "fair"ly good clue to help us learn about prayer. Microphones and loud speakers are important at fairs so that information can be communicated to fair contestants and to those who are visiting the fairground. Let's meet a fair contestant named Emily. As you listen to what Emily's doing at her county fair, see if you can understand why a microphone is important.**

Prayer at the Fair Opening Devotion

Hand out Resource Page 1. Select a volunteer to read it out loud.

Ask **How was a microphone used at Emily's county fair?** (To communicate that it was time for the contestants to be at the show-ring) **What danger does Emily face as she leads Flash into the show-ring?** (The horse's front legs are up and could possibly kick Emily.) **What did Emily do as soon as Flash reared up?** (Prayed to God) **Why did Emily pray to God?** (Emily trusts that God will hear her prayer and help her by protecting her from danger.)

Say **In our Bible account today, we will meet a man named Daniel. Daniel is also in a dangerous situation. We'll find out more about Daniel and his prayers to God. God always answers the prayers of His children. We'll find out how God answered Daniel's prayers.**

Offering Encourage the students as they give their offerings. If you have a special summer mission project, introduce it today. A suggestion is explained on the Director CD.

Pray **Dear heavenly Father, thank You for inviting us to talk to You in prayer. As we study Your Word today, give us trust in You that You hear and answer all our prayers. In Jesus' name we pray. Amen.**

Celebrate Recognize student birthdays, Baptism birthdays, and significant family events in your routine manner.

Teacher Tip

Each week, gather in the same location for the opening worship and closing activities. Lead your students each week in making the sign of the cross and saying the Invocation together.

2 God Speaks (20 minutes)

God Teaches about Prayer

To Prepare: Have Bibles available and copies of Student Leaflet 1.

Move to the Blue-Ribbon Bible Stories "arena."

Say **In our devotion, we heard Emily offer a prayer to God for help as she was ready to show her horse at the fair. In this Bible account, we will meet a man named Daniel who also needed God's help. Daniel and God's people were living in captivity in a country named Babylon.**

Ask **What does the word *captivity* mean?** (One group of people is forcing another group of people to live under them.)

Say **God loved His people but had allowed the Babylonians to take them captive as a punishment, because they had turned away from Him. God allowed this experience to happen to them so they would turn back to Him. While Daniel and the other Jewish people were living in Babylon, they had to follow what the Babylonian king told them to do or face punishment. Because of God's grace, Daniel worked for King Darius. But Daniel's faith put him in a difficult situation with the king.**

Direct the students to stand and face you.

Say **Today's Bible account is presented as an echo action story. Watch me carefully. After I say each line of the story, I will do an action to illustrate it. When I stop, you will repeat what I just said and did.**

Teacher Tip

The rhythm of this story is similar to a military cadence. Every two lines form a couplet. The first word or the first syllable of the first word in each line should be stressed. For example, the first couplet would go, "DAN-iel was a man of God, HELPED the king in Babylon."

Daniel was a man of God,	*Point upward.*
Helped the king in Babylon.	*Hold out hands, palms up.*
Daniel prayed three times a day.	*Fold hands in prayer.*
"Thank You, God," did Daniel say.	*Bow head in thanks.*
Jealous men devised a plot,	*Tap forehead with finger as if thinking.*
Wanted Dan to hurt a lot.	*Hold arm as if in pain.*
Darius they went to see,	*Walk in place.*
Asked this king for a decree.	*Shake fist.*
So the king told everyone,	*Cup hand in front of mouth.*
"Pray to me or you'll be done."	*Hang head.*
God's man Dan would not obey.	*Shake head no.*
Just to God would Daniel pray.	*Point upward, fold hands.*
Down into the lions' den	*Point downward.*
Went poor Dan—was this the end?	*Shrug shoulders.*
Stone door sealed the den quite tight.	*Pound right fist into left palm.*
Darius can't sleep all night.	*Pace in place.*
Early at the morn's first light,	*Shade eyes from sun.*
Darius feared a bad sight.	*Cover eyes in fear.*
To the den the king did go.	*Run in place.*
"Are you safe, Dan? Let me know."	*Cup hand to ear to listen.*
"I am safe," was his reply.	*Make "okay" sign with thumb/pointer.*
"God's my helper. I'm alive.	*Raise arms in praise.*
"(An) angel shut the lions' mouths.	*Clap hands once, hold palms together.*
"God saved me, I have no doubts!"	*Raise hands in praise.*
God heard Daniel's ev'ry prayer.	*Fold hands in prayer.*

God showed Dan His awesome care.	*Hug self.*
Darius told all the land,	*Cup hands to mouth as if shouting.*
"Honor the God of this man!"	*Point toward heaven.*

Review

Hand out Student Leaflet 1 and pencils. Have the students do the Search & Know activity on page 4 of the leaflet together. To further challenge students, have them reword the false statements to make them true. **Answers:** 1. True; 2. False; 3. False; 4. True; 5. True; 6. True; 7. False; 8. True; 9. True; 10. True.

Bible Words

In the day of my trouble I call upon You, for You answer me. Psalm 86:7

Locate the Bible Words on the student leaflet.

Say **In our Bible account, Daniel prayed to God three times a day.**

Print the Faith Word, *prayer*, on the board.

Ask **What does the Faith Word, *prayer*, mean?** (Prayer is speaking to God in words and thoughts.)

Ask **When he prayed, Daniel spoke to or called to God. How do you know that God heard Daniel's prayers?** (God saved Daniel from the lions.)

Say **In our Bible Words for today, we are reminded that when we talk to or call upon God, we can trust that God hears our prayers and answers them according to His will for our lives.**

Print the Bible verse on the board. Read it again. This time as you read it, point at yourself on the words *I*, *my*, and *me* and point up on the word *You.* Invite the students to imitate your actions as they say the verse. Then divide the class into three groups, standing in lines facing one another. Assign Group 1 the words, "In the day of my trouble." Assign Group 2 the words, "I call upon You." Assign Group 3 the words, "for You answer me." Challenge the groups to say the verse parts in order back and forth to one another while using the gestures taught earlier. Then have the groups switch verse parts and repeat the activity.

3 We Live (20 minutes)

Pray, Praise & Give Thanks

To Prepare: Make copies of Activity Page 1. Have pencils and Bibles available.

Say **Daniel had been given an important position by Babylon's King Darius. Other government officials were jealous of Daniel. They could find no fault with Daniel's work or the way he lived.**

Say **In order to bring Daniel down, what did they do?** (Manipulated Darius to create a law that forbid anyone to pray to anyone but him)

Ask **How did Daniel react to the new law?** (Daniel was faithful to the one true God. He continued to pray only to God, not to Darius.)

Ask **Why did Daniel continue to pray to God even though he knew he might die because of his faith?** (Daniel loved and honored God as the only true God. Daniel believed and trusted in God. Daniel knew that only the triune God has the power to hear prayer and to help and save.)

Ask **How did God save Daniel?** (God sent an angel. The lions' mouths were shut so they could not hurt Daniel.)

Ask **During devotions, we met a girl named Emily who was getting ready to show her horse at the fair. Why did Emily pray to God?** (Emily trusted that God would hear her prayer and help her to control Flash.)

Ask **What are some times that you and other people you know pray?** (Let students share. Answers include mealtimes, bedtime, when they wake up in the morning, during frightening situations, in illness, in church and Sunday School, before an athletic competition, before a difficult test at school, etc.)

Say **God has given us a relationship with Him through faith in Jesus. God gives us faith as we hear His Word and when we are baptized. As sinners who disobey God and who are born as God's enemies, we wouldn't have this relationship with God without Jesus. He suffered and died on the cross to pay the price we owed God for our sins. Jesus rose from the dead and conquered sin, death, and the devil for us. Through Him, we have been made right with God; He has restored our relationship with God the Father.**

Ask **What is very important to do when you have a friendship or relationship with someone?** (People need to communicate with one another.)

Say **Prayer is how we communicate with God. Prayer is speaking to God in words and thoughts. God listened to Daniel's prayers and saved him from the lions. Through Jesus, God has saved us from sin, death, and that lion, the devil. God promises to hear and to answer our prayers for Jesus' sake. Through His Word and Sacraments, God strengthens our faith so we can trust in His promises to hear our prayers and give us what we need. When God doesn't give us something we pray for, it means that He has a better plan for our life or the life of someone else, even though we may not be able to see that at the time.**

Teacher Tip

If time is limited, only complete the underlined numbers, which apply to today's Bible account. Finish the worksheet during next week's Bible lesson, "Jesus Heals the Centurion's Servant," or send it home for the children to complete as a preview to the concepts in that lesson.

Hand out Bibles, pencils, and Activity Page 1.

Say **The Bible tells us many things about prayer. Let's work this crossword puzzle and explore prayer together.**

Assign each child one verse to look up and read aloud. As students uncover each word for the puzzle from the Bible verses, print them on the board.

Puzzle answers: (Across) 3. People; 4. Faith; 5. Anything; 9. Answer; 11. Every place; 14. Deliver; 15. Persecute. (Down) 1. Supplication; 2. Circumstances; 6. Holy Spirit; 7. Prayed; 8. Triune; 10. Hear; 12. Will; 13. Jesus.

Craft—Prayer Wheel Passenger Pockets

To Prepare: Provide a 6 × 9-inch white envelope for each student. (Or adjust the size according to the size of your Ferris wheel.) Cut off the top (open end) using a curved path. See diagram. A 3-D option is to decorate small gift (favor) boxes with the top flaps cut off or tucked in. Instead of purchasing boxes, they can be made using an online pattern; just print, cut out, and assemble. Have pencils, crayons, markers, transparent tape, pipe cleaners, and self-adhesive plastic gems ready for use.

Say **We are going to use a Ferris wheel model to design a prayer wheel that we will use for lesson activities each week.**

Gesture toward the worship area you have set up in your classroom.

Ask **As you can see, a Ferris wheel base for our prayer wheel has already been set up in the worship place. But what's missing on this Ferris wheel?** (The passenger cars, called gondolas)

Hand out a precut envelope pocket to each student.

Say **These are prayer wheel passenger pockets. Let's decorate them to put on the prayer wheel. Use bold, bright colors to print your name on the front. Add a bright border around the envelope's edge.** They could tape back the bottom two corners to give the car a more "rounded" look. And they could tape a curved pipe cleaner at the top at each edge, forming a covered canopy to the car. When students are done, invite them to use masking tape to tape the back of the pocket to the end of a spoke and use self-adhesive plastic gems for decorating the spoke, representing lights.

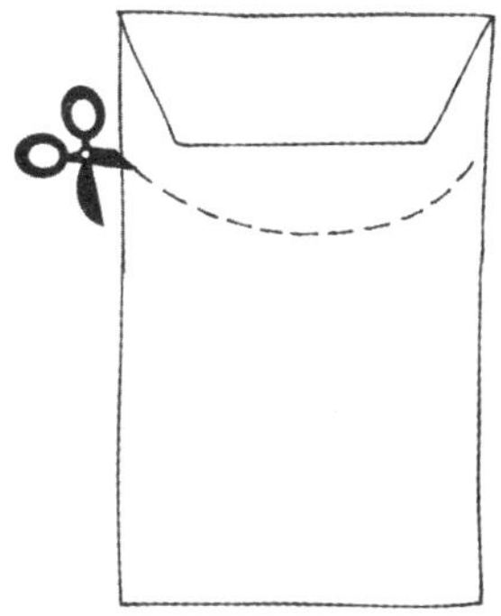

4 Closing (5 minutes)

To Prepare: Make sure students have their fair tickets with them. Also have the microphone available. Gather together in the worship area.

Sing "Children of the Heavenly Father" (*LSB* 725; Director CD 1) or "I Am Trusting Thee, Lord Jesus" (*LSB* 729).

Show the microphone and a Lesson 1 fair ticket.

Ask **What is today's "fair"ly good clue about prayer?** (A microphone)

Say **People use microphones at fairs and other events to make sure others can hear their message. Let's read together today's Take-Home Point on the tickets: God hears my prayers. We don't need to use any gadget to communicate with God. We don't even need to speak out loud. God knows and hears our words and thoughts whenever we pray. He promises to hear all our prayers and answer them according to His will, always doing what is best for us. Let's pray to God now.**

Pray **Heavenly Father, You are so good to us! We thank You for the love, forgiveness, and protection You give us. We especially thank You for protecting us from sin, death, and the devil through Jesus. Help us to pray only to You. Strengthen our faith in You so we trust that You always hear and answer us. In Jesus' name and for His sake we pray. Amen.**

Direct the students to put their Lesson 1 fair ticket into their prayer wheel pocket. As each person leaves, say, **God hears your prayers.**

Snack

Popping Corn

Popcorn is a popular snack at a fair. Make popcorn in your classroom using an air or oil popper, or prepare microwave popcorn if one is available. As the popcorn cooks, have the students listen to the sounds the exploding kernels make. Remind them that God hears all our prayers. (In fact, the Bible teaches that God knows what we are going to pray even before we think or say the words!)

Living the Faith

Encourage the students in the coming week to include in their prayers Christians around the world who currently face punishment and even death because of their faith in the one true God. Encourage them to ask God to give these fellow believers boldness in prayer and courage and hope in the truth that they have eternal life through faith in Jesus.

All about Prayer

Directions: Locate and read each Bible verse. Find the word from the verse that is needed to answer each puzzle clue. Solve the crossword puzzle by placing the missing words you find into their correct places. If time is limited, first complete the underlined numbers, then complete the rest later.

CLUES

Across

3. We should pray for all of these (1 Timothy 2:1)
4. If you have this, whatever you ask for in prayer you will receive (Matthew 21:22)
5. If we pray according to God's will, we can ask Him for this (1 John 5:14)
9. Another thing God promises to do when we pray to Him (Isaiah 65:24)
11. Where we can pray (1 Timothy 2:8)
14. What God promises to do for us when we pray to Him when we are in trouble (Psalm 50:15)
15. Jesus tells us to pray for those people who do this to us (Matthew 5:44)

Down

1. A prayer made for a specific need (1 Timothy 2:1)
2. We should pray in all of these (1 Thessalonians 5:18)
6. This person of the triune God helps us to pray (Romans 8:26)
7. What Daniel did to talk to God despite the king's decree (Daniel 6:10)
8. The only God to whom we pray (2 Corinthians 13:14)
10. When we pray to Him, God promises to do this (1 John 5:14)
12. We are to pray according to this of God's (1 John 5:14)
13. In this name we should pray (John 16:23)

Lesson 2

Preparing the Lesson

Jesus Heals the Centurion's Servant

Matthew 8:5–13—God tells me to pray for everything.

Key Point

The centurion prayed for his servant to be healed. God invites us to pray for our needs and the needs of others.

Law/**Gospel**

The result of sin is sickness, suffering, and death (Genesis 3:15–19), which can sometimes manifest itself in birth defects, hereditary diseases, communicable illnesses, paralysis, mental illness, and physical injuries. **Jesus died for sin once for all, redeeming both soul and body. He invites me to pray for both spiritual and bodily blessings for myself and others in need, and on the Last Day, He will raise me and all who believe in Him to life eternal with glorified, perfect bodies.**

Context

Jesus had begun His earthly ministry of preaching, teaching, and working miracles. His preaching revolves around repentance and forgiveness (Matthew 4:17). He had already called His disciples and preached the Sermon on the Mount. "The crowds were astonished at His teaching, for He was teaching them as one who had authority" (Matthew 7:28–29). When He came down from the mountain, He healed a leper and then entered into Capernaum, a city on the Sea of Galilee, His home district.

Commentary

A centurion is a Roman military officer in command of one hundred soldiers. The Romans were an occupying army. They were not Jewish. For the most part, they did not sympathize with the Jewish religion. This officer approaches Jesus, interceding on behalf of his paralyzed servant. His care and concern for his servant is admirable.

Jesus agrees to come to the centurion's house in order to heal the servant. But the officer objects, citing his own unworthiness for Jesus to enter into his house. He knows that like the leper, he is an outcast in Jewish society. He understands that Jewish customs are different from Roman customs and that he is considered unclean. He also understands that Jesus is a holy man and that he himself is a sinner. Therefore, he says, "Lord, I am not worthy to have You come under my roof." This is a profound and unusual confession from a high-ranking Roman officer.

His next confession is more impressive. "Only say the word, and my servant will be healed" (8:8). Here, he shows that he also understands that Jesus has the authority to command supernatural forces. The centurion believes that Jesus has divine power to heal without being present. He comprehends that his military authority is a small picture of God's eternal authority here on earth.

Marveling at the man's faith, Jesus takes the opportunity to reprimand the Jews for their lack of repentance and faith. A foreigner comes to Jesus in faith seeking divine mercy, but His own people refuse to believe.

The Gospel of Jesus is not for the Jews only; it is for all people, regardless of nationality or race, who have faith that Jesus is Lord. This faith is demonstrated by willingness to confess unworthiness for God's grace, trust in God's power, and confidence to approach God in prayer.

Jesus grants the centurion's petition, and his servant is healed that very moment.

Prayer is intercession for yourself and others. Matthew, Mark, Luke, and John record for us how Jesus often prayed. The content of those prayers shows that He prayed not only for what was about to happen to Him, but also for His disciples and those who would listen to them (John 17:20–21).

A noteworthy part of Paul's letters is his admission that he prays for the people to whom he is writing and asks them to pray for him as well. He tells Timothy to make petitions for all people, for kings and all those in authority. Those who believe in Jesus can pray to God not only for themselves but also for others, even unbelievers, and expect God to hear them for Jesus' sake.

To hear an in-depth discussion of this Bible account, visit cph.org/podcast and listen to our Seeds of Faith podcast each week.

Lesson 2

Jesus Heals the Centurion's Servant

Matthew 8:5–13

Connections

Bible Words
I urge that supplications, prayers, intercessions, and thanksgivings be made for all people. 1 Timothy 2:1

Faith Word
intercession

Hymns and Songs
The King's Kids Are Prayin' (Director CD 9)

Come, My Soul, with Every Care (*LSB* 779; Director CD 2)

Children of the Heavenly Father (*LSB* 725; Director CD 1)

We Pray For Each Other (Director CD 12)

Catechism
We should ask for everything that tends to the glory of God and to our own and our neighbor's welfare, both spiritual and bodily blessings. (Question 197)

Take-Home Point
God tells me to pray for everything.

1 Opening (15 minutes)

Welcome

To Prepare: Before class, make copies of the Lesson 2 fair ticket from the Director CD. Place these tickets behind the ticket booth window. Have extra envelopes available for students who still need to make a prayer wheel pocket craft to add to the class Ferris wheel (Lesson 1). Make copies of "A Responsive Reading on Prayer" (Director CD or p. 12)and Resource Page 2.

Sit behind the ticket window and greet students. Pass out Lesson 2 tickets.

Say **Welcome back to the Christian County Fair and to our Sunday School course, *Pray, Praise & Give Thanks: Jesus Teaches Us to Pray.* We will explore Bible stories that focus on prayer and stories that teach the Lord's Prayer. Each week our fair has a special theme. Let's read today's theme found on your ticket: God tells me to pray for everything. Let's begin with song and prayer.** Move to the worship area of your classroom.

Worship

Sing "The King's Kids Are Prayin'" (Director CD 9) or "Come, My Soul, with Every Care" (*LSB* 779; Director CD 2). God invites us pray for all things.

Invocation **In the name of the Father and of the Son and of the Holy Spirit. Amen.**

Hand out copies of "A Responsive Reading on Prayer" (Director CD or p. 12).

MATERIALS NEEDED

1 Opening	2 God Speaks	3 We Live	4 Closing
Director CD Lesson 2 fair tickets (Director CD) Copies of "A Responsive Reading on Prayer" (Director CD or p. 12) Resource Page 2 Red Cross symbol poster	Bibles Student Leaflet 2	Bibles Activity Page 2 Lesson 2 fair ticket Wreath ring pattern (Director CD) Cardstock paper in bright colors or cardboard pizza circles Construction paper Masking tape	Director CD Lesson 2 fair tickets Current list of congregational illnesses from church bulletin or other resource Index cards (1 each)

Say **Every week we will use this reading to help us learn more about what it means to pray to our triune God.** Use the reading together.

A "Fair"ly Good Clue to Learn a Fact about Prayer

Say **Take out the ticket you received when you entered the main gate earlier today. Find the red cross.**

Ask **What does this symbol represent?** (This is the Red Cross symbol. It marks where people can receive medical attention in a safe place. This symbol is recognized by people all around the world, no matter where they live or what language they speak.)

Ask **Where is the Red Cross symbol posted on your ticket?** (It's on a tent.)

Say **Why do you think a first-aid tent is an important feature at fairs?** (Injuries and illnesses can happen due to heat, working with animals, and other circumstances. The Red Cross sign lets everyone know that the tent is a place where they can receive medical help.)

Web Activity: Locate an appropriate website providing basic information on the International Red Cross. Note the medical work they do in times of emergency and crisis. As always, preview websites before class.

Prayer at the Fair Opening Devotion

Ask **You'll recall in our first lesson that we heard about a girl named Emily who is participating in the horse show at her county fair. What happened to Emily as she was waiting to enter the show-ring with Flash?** (Something spooked Flash and caused him to rear up on his hind legs. Emily prayed to God and asked Him for help and protection.)

Say **Let's read about what happens next to Emily and Flash.**

Hand out Resource Page 2. Invite volunteers to read the story.

Ask **How did God answer Emily's prayers for help?** (God gave Emily the ability to calm Flash so he could participate in the show. Through faith, God led Hannah to pray for care for Emily's injury. God can work through the medics at the first-aid tent to tend to Emily's injured hand.)

Ask **In our last lesson, we talked about what prayer is. What is prayer?** (Prayer is speaking to God in words and thoughts.)

Say **Through faith, Emily and Hannah prayed to God and trusted that He would answer their prayers. They knew that they could pray to God to help them in every kind of trouble. In our Bible account today, we will hear about a Roman soldier who needed some "red cross help" for his servant. As we study this Bible story, we will discover why this soldier prayed to Jesus in his time of need.**

Offering Encourage the students as they give their offerings. Offerings are used to help others in need.

Pray **Dear heavenly Father, bless our time together today in Your Word. As we explore a miracle of Jesus, help us to see that we can pray to You for everything and that You promise to hear and answer all our prayers. In Jesus' name we pray. Amen.**

Celebrate Recognize student birthdays, Baptism birthdays, and significant family events in your routine manner.

2 God Speaks (20 minutes)

God Teaches about Prayer

To Prepare: Have Bibles, pencils, and Student Leaflet 2 ready for use.

Gather together in the Blue-Ribbon Bible Stories arena.

Say **During the time when Jesus lived here on earth, the area in which He and the Jewish people lived was ruled by the Roman government. The Romans had stationed soldiers throughout the land to keep the peace among the people and to see that taxes were collected. They were not Jewish. For the most part, members of the Roman army did not understand or support the Jewish religion. The Romans often had conflicts with the ruling council of the Jewish temple in Jerusalem.**

In the Bible account that we are about to read, Jesus is approached by a Roman centurion. A *centurion* is a Roman military officer in command of one hundred soldiers. This account takes place in Capernaum, a city located on the northwest shore of the Sea of Galilee.

Select one person to read the part of the centurion in the Bible story (Matthew 8:6, 8–9) and another person to read Jesus' words (Matthew 8:7, 10–12, 13). If desired, have them stand "on stage." You and the rest of the students will serve as narrators, reading the rest of the story out loud together, describing what happened. At the proper points in the Bible story, cue the actors playing the centurion and Jesus to read their dialogue directly from the Bible. (It may help to write their verse references on the board, so they can highlight them ahead of time.)

Hand out Bibles. Help students to locate Matthew 8:5–13 as necessary. Invite the actors playing the centurion and Jesus to act out the Bible story in front of the class. If necessary, explain the meaning of the word *paralyzed*.

Review

Hand out Student Leaflet 2 and pencils. Have the students do the Search & Know activity on page 4 to review the lesson details. Work together as a class to complete the story version as you use the words in the Word Box. **Answers** (in the order they appear): centurion, servant, paralyzed, heal, worthy, word, soldiers, Israel, faith, believed, healed, moment.

Bible Words

I urge that supplications, prayers, intercessions, and thanksgivings be made for all people. 1 Timothy 2:1

Locate the Bible Words on the student leaflet. Read them out loud together.

Say **The words *supplications, intercessions,* and *thanksgivings* are all types of prayers we can pray.**

Print the Faith Word, *intercession*, on the board.

Say **Intercessions are prayers we pray to God for others and their needs. Who prayed an intercession in today's Bible account?** (Centurion) **For whom did the centurion pray?** (His paralyzed servant who was suffering)

Print the four words on the board: *supplications*, *prayers*, *intercessions*, and *thanksgivings*. Number the words 1 through 4. Divide the class into four small groups, each assigned a number and one word. As you say the verse, have each group stand and say the word on the board with their number, then quickly sit back down. Only you or one group should talk at a time. Repeat this activity several times. Then say it again several times, inviting everyone to stand up and say the last phrase "be made for all people" together at the same time, emphasizing the idea that we pray for everyone (and everything).

3 We Live (20 minutes)

Pray, Praise & Give Thanks

To Prepare: Have copies of Activity Page 2, Bibles, pencils, and a lesson ticket.

Say **The account of the centurion and Jesus has much to tell us about prayer, faith, and who Jesus is. Let's explore more about this.**

Ask **Earlier we discussed that the Roman soldiers and the Jewish people did not get along well or share the same faith in God. What was unusual about this centurion?** (He knew Jesus and believed/trusted in Jesus' power and authority to heal his servant. It was also unusual that he would even think to pray for his paralyzed servant.)

Ask **How did Jesus answer the centurion's prayer?** (He healed the servant.)

Ask **What was miraculous about the way in which Jesus healed the man?** (Jesus did not even need to be near the servant in order to heal him.)

Ask **In many Bibles, the title for this event is "The Faith of a Centurion." Why is this a good title?** (Through faith, the centurion trusted that Jesus had the power to heal his servant.)

Ask **Why didn't the centurion want Jesus to come into his home?** (The centurion told Jesus that he was unworthy to have Him come under his roof. His faith allowed him to recognize his unworthiness in the presence of the Christ. In terms of the local culture, the centurion was an outsider because he was not Jewish. According to Jewish law, the centurion's home was an unclean place for Jesus to be.)

Ask **Jesus was willing, however, to come to the centurion's home and heal his servant. What does this tell you about Jesus?** (Jesus came not just for the Jews, but also for the Gentiles, all people who are not of the Jewish race and faith. Read 1 Timothy 2:4. God wants all people to be saved.)

Ask **Jesus came for *all* people. That includes you and me. Why do we need Jesus?** (We need Jesus because we sin and are all spiritually sick. We suffer from the results of sin: sickness, suffering, and death. We may not be physically sick ourselves, but we may be sad because of the sicknesses of others, like the centurion who had sympathy for his paralyzed servant.)

Ask **Jesus invites us to pray for spiritual and physical blessings for ourselves and for others. How does Jesus heal us?** (Jesus died for sin once for all. Through Jesus' death and resurrection, He redeemed both our soul and our bodies. On the Last Day, imperfect physical bodies of all believers will be raised and restored, glorified and perfect.)

Show the Red Cross symbol on a Lesson 2 ticket.

Ask **How is a red cross an important symbol for people who believe in Jesus?** (It reminds us that Jesus listens to the prayers for the needs of everyone and everything. The medical red cross is universally recognized to mark places where *all people* can receive help. The red cross reminds us that Jesus shed His blood on the cross so that *all people* might be saved from death.)

Hand out pencils and Activity Page 2.

Say **God tells us to pray for everything, according to His will for our lives. As our Bible verse and Faith Word for this lesson tells us, we can pray intercessions—prayers for others and their needs. In this fair scene, there are several people for whom we can pray. Let's talk together about these individuals and some needs of theirs about which we can intercede. Make some notes about these needs on the lines next to each situation.** Encourage student responses.

Teacher Tip

As you discuss illness, empathetically discuss that while we still live on earth, God sometimes allows us to remain sick for reasons known only to Himself, or He may allow a Christian to die and be taken to heaven, where that person will no longer suffer pain or illness. The fact that we are Christians and have faith does not mean that God will always heal us, but He will do what is best for us and wants us to pray to Him for healing when we need it.

Ask **Let's find the Ferris wheel and the worker operating it. About what might we pray for this person and for the people enjoying this ride?** (Safety for the riders, fun for the riders, skillful hands and eyes for the worker to load the riders properly and to watch for any safety concerns, etc.)

Ask **Find the child who has dropped some ice cream. How might we pray for this child and his dad?** (Comfort for the child, patience for the dad, etc.)

Ask **Find the girl and her sheep in the animal barn. About what might we pray in this situation?** (Knowledge for the girl as to the proper way to care for her sheep, health for both the girl and her livestock, thanks for God's providence and care, etc.)

Ask **Finally, locate the mom and the child with the hurt arm. About what might we pray in this situation?** (Healing for the child, skill for the medical people treating the child, love and kindness and peace and a calm spirit for the mom as she cares for her injured child, etc.)

Craft—Prayer Reminder Wreath

To Prepare: Copy the wreath base pattern (Director CD) onto cardstock (ideally, colored) or provide a clean cardboard pizza circle base for each child. Cut out the inside, leaving just a ring, or give children time and assistance to do so during class. Provide many different colors of construction paper, as well as pencils, dark-colored markers, scissors, and glue sticks.

Say **God tells us to pray for everything. Let's make prayer reminder wreaths to remind us of the many things about which we can pray to God. To begin, let's make a list of situations, blessings, and people for whom we can pray.** As students mention ideas, write them on the board.

Work together as a class to compile a list of physical and spiritual needs (e.g., food, clothing, health, parents, grandparents, teachers, pastors, firefighters, police officers, homes, safety, a strong faith, forgiveness, boldness to share Jesus with others). Give each child a pencil, scissors, dark-colored marker, and several sheets of one color of paper.

Say **Use a pencil to trace your hand on one of your papers. Stack the papers and cut out several hands at a time.** Model how to align the corners of the paper; tape together if necessary to avoid movement during cutting.

You may want them to fold the paper in half to cut two hands at a time, or cut the paper in half, so they are working with a smaller piece of paper.

Say **Keep one of your hands and trade the rest with other students, so that you end up with many different hand colors and sizes. Select ideas from the prayer list on the board and write one on each hand. Decorate the wreath base by evenly spacing out and gluing the bottom of each hand onto it. Keep the fingers pointing out, and leave a little space between each hand. Use masking tape to display the prayer wreaths.**

4 Closing (5 minutes)

To Prepare: Have on hand a current list of those in your congregation who are ill. Provide an index card and pencil for each student. Students need their Lesson 2 fair ticket. Gather together in the worship area.

Sing "We Pray for Each Other" (Director CD 12) or "Children of the Heavenly Father" (*LSB* 725; Director CD 1).

Bring out a Lesson 2 fair ticket.

Say **Let's read today's theme: God tells me to pray for everything.** Point to the Red Cross symbol on the tent. **This red cross can remind us that God wants us to pray not only for our needs but also for the needs of others, especially when they are sick, like when the centurion prayed for his servant in today's lesson.**

Bring out the list of those who are ill.

Say **There are many individuals in our church family, in our community, in our nation, and throughout the world who are suffering from illnesses of many kinds. We may not personally know these people, but these are all people for whom we can pray.** Share some names of the people on the lists you've gathered. Then give an index card and pencil to each person.

Say **On your index card, write down the first name of someone you know who has some *health needs* about which we can pray. Then on the back of the card, write down the first name of someone you know who has a *spiritual need* about which we can pray. For example, think of someone who doesn't go to church, someone who may not know Jesus is his or her Savior, or someone whose faith is weak. At a special time in our closing prayer, read the names of the people off your card.**

Pray **Dear Jesus, we know that You have the power to help us with all things. As You have invited us to pray for everything, today we pray for these people who need Your physical and spiritual healing help:** (Call students by name and direct them to read the names on their index card.) **Jesus, please be with these people we have named, and if it be Your will, restore their health. In Your name we pray. Amen.**

Direct the students to place their ticket into their prayer wheel pocket. Make sure they take their prayer cards home with them. As each child leaves, say, **God tells us to pray for everything.**

Living the Faith

Encourage the students to continue to pray throughout the week for the people they named on their index card during the lesson closing.

Snack

Food on a Stick

Jesus was hung on a wooden cross to suffer and die so we wouldn't have to. Fairs are famous for offering a variety of items served on a wooden stick. Serve precut chunks of fresh fruit, such as watermelon, grapes, apples, and pineapple, on bamboo skewers. The same idea can be used with vegetable chunks of zucchini, cucumber, carrots, and cherry tomatoes. Small squares of coffee cake, sweet rolls, or doughnut holes can also be skewered and served. Closely supervise activities that involve a sharp object.

Directions: Look carefully at the people in the fair scene below. On the lines near each of the people, write down a need they might have for which you can pray.

Lesson 3

Preparing the Lesson

Peter and John Heal a Lame Man

Acts 3:1–10—God is worthy of my thanks and praise.

Key Point

The lame man praised and thanked God. We pray, praise, and give thanks to God for who He is and what He has done for us through His Son, Jesus.

Law/**Gospel**

Sin renders me helpless so that I look to myself or to the sinful world around me, to money or possessions, to make me whole instead of looking to God. **God heals my diseases and cleanses me from the sickness of sin for the sake of His Son, Jesus, who paid for all my sins on the cross. Renewed in spirit, I respond with praise and thanks for what God has done.**

Context

Jesus has ascended into heaven. He departed, telling His disciples to wait in Jerusalem for the coming of the Holy Spirit. On Pentecost, the Spirit came, giving the disciples the ability to preach the Gospel with great ability and confidence. The Christian Church began to grow on account of this preaching. People were being baptized and gathering to hear the apostles' teaching and to partake of the Lord's Supper (Acts 2:42). Many were being saved.

Commentary

The disciples had the custom of going to the temple at regular hours to pray. These outward customs for prayer did not end when Jesus died, rose, and ascended. In fact, many of the first Christian prayer disciplines came from Jewish practices. While learning of Jesus through the apostles, new believers still retained the practice of meeting and praying together (Acts 2:42-43). The Christian Church adopted specific days and times for prayer similar to Jewish tradition. They continued to use the Psalms to guide their prayers and even sang psalms and songs in the way they had learned them in the temple.

As Peter and John approached the temple for prayer, the lame man begging outside the Beautiful Gate asked them for alms (money), but they had none to give him. However, Peter's compassion prompted him to work a miracle in the name of Jesus.

The Holy Spirit had filled the apostles with the ability to work miracles of healing. The Book of Acts attests to the apostles, and those with them, working "signs and wonders," or what we would call miracles (2:43; 5:12; 6:8; 14:3; 15:12). This was a peculiar ability that the Holy Spirit gave to the apostles. On this occasion, Peter and John gave the man something more precious than silver or gold. In the name of Jesus of Nazareth, they commanded the man to stand up and walk. Then they took him by the hand and he stood, being healed.

The beggar wanted a little money to help him live but ended up with much more than he asked for, receiving bodily healing instead. The man knew that he had been healed by a supernatural action and rightly attributed it to the Lord working through Peter and John. After being healed, he went with them into the temple to praise God. This was a wonderful testimony for those around him that the Lord had healed him.

Luther's meaning to the Second Commandment tells us not only how to keep from misusing God's name but also how to use it rightly. God wants to be called upon when we or our neighbors are in need. He also wants us to praise and give thanks to Him for blessings that He has given us. This is not because God is in need of our praise and thanks. He lacks nothing. We do not add to God with our praise. However, in a way only our Lord could know, we are blessed again by our praise and thanks. It changes us. Our praise increases our faith in God, who gives all good things.

To hear an in-depth discussion of this Bible account, visit cph.org/podcast and listen to our Seeds of Faith podcast each week.

Lesson 3

Peter and John Heal a Lame Man

Acts 3:1–10

Connections

Bible Words
Give thanks to the Lord, for He is good, for His steadfast love endures forever. Psalm 136:1

Faith Word
worthy

Hymns and Songs
The King's Kids Are Prayin' (Director CD 9)

Silver and Gold (*AGPS* 212:1)

Children of the Heavenly Father (*LSB* 725; Director CD 1)

We Praise You, O God (*LSB* 785; Director CD 11)

Catechism
We should also praise and thank God for who He is and what He has done. (Question 197)

Take-Home Point
God is worthy of my thanks and praise.

1 Opening (15 minutes)

Welcome

To Prepare: Before class, make copies of the Lesson 3 fair ticket (Director CD). Have copies of "A Responsive Reading on Prayer" (Director CD or p. 12) available. Obtain an actual blue ribbon awarded at a fair, or purchase one.

Special Event: If you have any current or former 4-H or FFA members in your congregation, invite them to attend the Opening today and bring any projects they have made or photos of their projects, along with any ribbons they have won. You may want to set up a table for displaying them.

Sit behind the ticket window and greet students. Pass out Lesson 3 tickets.

Say **Welcome back to the Christian County Fair and to our Sunday School course, *Pray, Praise & Give Thanks: Jesus Teaches Us to Pray.* We are exploring Bible stories that focus on prayer and that teach about the Lord's Prayer. Let's read together today's fair theme found at the bottom of your ticket: God is worthy of my thanks and praise.**

Introduce the special guests you've invited. **Come over to our exhibitors' table and see the prizes these individuals have won.** Give the students some time to view the projects and ask the guests questions.

Web Activity: Particularly if you don't have special guests, search "4-H county fair awards [your county or state]" to see winners/exhibits in your area, or search online with the key words "blue-ribbon winning recipe" or "vegetable" or "animal." Preview before class.

Thank your guests for coming. Move to the worship area of your room.

MATERIALS NEEDED

1 Opening	2 God Speaks	3 We Live	4 Closing
Director CD Lesson 3 fair tickets (Director CD) Copies of "A Responsive Reading on Prayer" (Director CD or p. 12) Resource Page 3 Blue ribbon (actual award from a fair or from a store) Special guests to visit classroom (optional) Extra table (optional)	Bibles Student Leaflet 3	Bibles Activity Page 3 Blue-Ribbon God pattern (Director CD) White cardstock Blue crepe paper	Director CD Lesson 3 fair tickets

Worship

Sing "The King's Kids Are Prayin'" (Director CD 9) or "We Praise You, O God" (*LSB* 785; Director CD 11). God is worthy of our praise as our Lord and King!

Invocation **In the name of the Father and of the Son and of the Holy Spirit. Amen.**

Hand out copies of "A Responsive Reading on Prayer" (Director CD or p. 12).

Use the reading together.

A "Fair"ly Good Clue to Learn a Fact about Prayer

Show the students the blue ribbon you have brought to class.

Ask **Why does someone receive a blue ribbon?** (He or she did the best job in an event or contest. Fair judges deem a person is worthy of a blue ribbon because he or she worked hard and was dedicated to his or her project.)

Say **Take out your ticket. Find the award ribbon image. Fair contestants hope to win ribbons, especially blue ones, in events they enter.**

Prayer at the Fair Opening Devotion

Ask **In our first two lessons, we met a girl named Emily and her horse, Flash. You will recall Emily suffered an injury to her hand, but she hoped to be back in time to show Flash. Let's find out what happened.**

Hand out Resource Page 3. Invite volunteers to read the story.

Ask **What did Emily and her parents pray for before she entered the show-ring?** (They thanked God for watching over Emily, healing her hand, and making Emily able to show Flash to the best of her ability.)

Ask **Why did Emily call Flash a "blue-ribbon horse" even though she doesn't yet know if she has won a blue ribbon?** (Flash correctly did all the maneuvers Emily had trained him to do. Emily believes his performance is worthy of a blue ribbon. She likes him the best, even if he's not scored best.)

Say **We have a blue-ribbon God. The triune God is the one and only true God, who is worthy of our thanks and praise. In this lesson's Bible account, we will find out about a man who gives God thanks and praise for a blessing that only God Himself could give.**

Offering Offerings give thanks to God for all of His blessings. Encourage students to return thanks.

Pray **Dear God, You are truly the very best! In You, all things are possible. As we study Your Word, help us to give You thanks and praise for all You have done and continue to do in our lives. In Jesus' name we pray. Amen.**

Celebrate Recognize student birthdays, Baptism birthdays, and significant family events in your routine manner.

2 God Speaks (20 minutes)

God Teaches about Prayer

To Prepare: Have Bibles, pencils, and Student Leaflet 3 ready for use.

Gather together in the Blue-Ribbon Bible Stories arena. Hand out Bibles.

Say **Turn to Acts 3:1–10. As I read out loud this Bible account, I will have several of you act out the section I just read, but without talking. I'll also ask questions along the way, so listen carefully.** Read verses 1–2.

Ask **The word *lame* can have several different meanings. Think about how the man got to the Beautiful Gate of the temple. What does *lame* mean in this Bible account?** (Although some people use the word to describe something stupid or boring, here it means the man couldn't walk.)

Ask two volunteers to come "on stage" and pantomime moving the lame man to the temple gate and laying him down. Ask a volunteer to play the part of the man who was lame. Have him lie down on the floor in the center.

Ask **The Bible tells us that the man who could not walk lay at the Beautiful Gate of the temple every day and asked for alms from the people who entered the temple. What are alms?** (Money that was given to help those in need) **Why did the man need to ask for money like this?** (Since he couldn't walk, he couldn't work. People entering the temple had pity for the man and gave him money so he could eat and survive.)

Direct the actor who is playing the lame man to hold out his hand as if begging. Then read verses 3–4 out loud. After you do so, select two other students to play the parts of Peter and John. Direct them to pantomime walking up to the lame man. Invite them to stand next to him "on stage."

Ask **What did the lame man ask Peter and John?** (He asked them for alms.) **What did Peter and John do after he asked for money?** (Both men looked at the lame man and asked him to look at them.)

Direct Peter and John to pantomime a motion that directs the lame man to look at them. Now read verses 5–6 out loud.

Ask **What did the lame man expect from Peter and John?** (Money) **Instead, what did Peter do?** (Peter told the man that he had no money, but he did have something to give him. Then he said, "In the name of Jesus Christ of Nazareth, rise up and walk!" (v. 6).

Read verse 7. Direct Peter to take the right hand of the lame man and gently help him to a standing position.

Ask **Who made the lame man's feet and ankles strong so that he could walk?** (Jesus' power miraculously healed the lame man.)

Read verse 8. Direct the lame man to walk and leap around.

Ask **As the once lame man could now walk and even leap, what else did he do? What was his first instinct after being healed by God's power?** (The man praised God.) **Why didn't the man praise Peter and John for his healing?** (Through the Holy Spirit working faith in him, he knew that no person could have healed him, only our all-powerful God. Filled with wonder

Teacher Tip

Provide context for the story. Today's Bible account takes place after Jesus ascended into heaven. On Pentecost, the Holy Spirit came and spoke through the disciples so they could powerfully preach the Gospel. By the power of the Holy Spirit, many people came to faith in Jesus. Peter and John and Jesus' other disciples went to the temple at regular hours to pray. They used the Psalms in the Bible to guide their prayers. Our Bible account begins as Peter and John were going to pray at the temple in Jerusalem at the "hour of prayer, the ninth hour" (Acts 3:1), which would have been 3:00 p.m.

and gratitude, the man joyfully praised God for his miraculous healing.)

As he continues to leap, direct the once lame man to also raise his hands in prayerful praise and thanks to God for healing. Then read verses 9–10.

Ask **When all the people saw the man now able to walk, how did they feel?** (They were filled with wonder and amazement.)

Direct all the other students to pantomime amazed facial expressions.

Review

Hand out Student Leaflet 3 and pencils. Encourage the students to individually work on the Search & Know activity on page 4 to review the lesson details. **Answers:** 1. c; 2. b; 3. b; 4. a; 5. a; 6. c; 7. b.

Bible Words

Give thanks to the Lord, for He is good, for His steadfast love endures forever.
Psalm 136:1

Locate the Bible Words on the student leaflet. Read them out loud together.

Ask **This Bible verse tells us two important things about God. What are they?** (God is good and His love for us never ends.) **He cares for us *always*. What does this verse tell us to do because God is good and because He always loves us?** (Give God thanks.) **He always gives us what's best!**

Print the Faith Word, *worthy*, on the board.

Ask **What does it mean to be worthy?** (To be deserving of something) **Why is God worthy of our thanks and praise?** (God is worthy because He does all things for us, including saving us from our sins and giving us eternal life. He deserves the credit; we don't do anything to earn our salvation.)

Divide the class into groups of three children each. Assign each person in each group a different verse part, based on the commas in the verse. When each person knows his or her part well, direct each group to stand in a separate line, one person behind the other. The first person in each line should be the person who has memorized the first part of the verse, the second person memorized the second part, and so on.

When you say, **One**, the first person in each trio says the first part of the verse, "Give thanks to the Lord," then goes to the end of their group's line. Repeat the process with the second and third in each line saying their part. Repeat the verse several times, each time challenging the students to go faster. Finally, have everyone stand still and say the entire verse together.

3 We Live (20 minutes)

Pray, Praise & Give Thanks

To Prepare: Make copies of Activity Page 3. Have Bibles and pencils available.

Ask **In this lesson's Bible account, how do Peter and John show the lame man mercy even though they don't give him any money?** (They show the man kindness and compassion by healing him in the name of Jesus.)

Ask **Why does each person in the world need mercy from God?** (We need God's mercy because we are helplessly lame in our sins. We think that on our own or with our own money or things we have, we will be healthy and whole, but we are sick with the disease of sin. The lame man couldn't make himself walk. And on our own, we can't stop the crippling effect sin has on us. Without God, we'd be stuck in sin, looking in the wrong places for help.)

Ask **How does God show us mercy?** (Even though we don't deserve God's love because we sin against Him, God still loves us. He loves us so much that He sent His Son, Jesus, to pay the price we owed for our sins, through His death on the cross. Through Jesus' resurrection, we are cleansed of our sins and healed. We praise and thank Him for who He is and for what He does for us!) Point to the word *worthy* on the board.

Say **Today's fair theme is "God is worthy of my thanks and praise." *Worthy* means that God is deserving of our thanks and praise because He is our Creator and Redeemer and the one who gives us faith in Him.**

Hand out Activity Page 3.

Say **Here are Bible verses that describe God and remind us why He is worthy of praise. Let's see what each one says about our champion God.**

Work together to find each Bible passage listed on the ribbons. Have the students write a characteristic of God inside the circle as described in the verse.

Answers: Malachi 3:6 God is unchanging. (Discuss that this means we can always depend on Him and on what He says. He keeps His promises. Because of Jesus, He will never change His mind or take away the salvation won for us.)

Genesis 17:1 God is almighty. (Discuss that this means God is all-powerful and is capable of doing anything. The Latin word for this is *omnipotent*.)

John 21:17 God is all-knowing/all-wise. (The Latin word for this is *omniscient*. When we pray to Him and even before we begin praying, God knows our thoughts, even when we don't speak them. He knows everything about every person in the world. His wisdom is so much greater than any person's.)

Jeremiah 23:24 God is everywhere. (The Latin word for this is *omnipresent*. No person can be in two places at a time. But God is everywhere at all times.)

Leviticus 19:2 God is holy. (This means God is sinless and that He hates sin.)

1 John 4:8 God is love. (God shows His love for us in everything He has done and continues to do for us. God loves us even when we are unlovable. God shows His love for us through Jesus, who cleanses us from our sin.)

Craft—Our Blue-Ribbon God

To Prepare: Each child will need the completed Activity Page 3 and two strips of blue crepe paper, a one-foot strip and a two-foot strip. Set out several copies of the Blue-Ribbon God pattern (Director CD) on white cardstock, though you probably won't need one per child. Provide scissors and transparent tape.

Say **Let's make and decorate blue ribbons to praise and thank God for who He is. We'll make life-size blue ribbons of the ones on Activity Page 3. Select one of the names or qualities of God that we uncovered as we explored the Bible verses. Use scissors to cut that characteristic from the pattern page, to be used as the circle area of the ribbon.**

To make the ribbon, first make a rosette for the top of the award. Start folding your long crepe-paper strip using an accordion fold. Make good creases. After a few folds, tape the folded end to your table. Continue to make folds by pinching up a small piece of the crepe paper, then folding. As you work, keep your thumb and index finger pinching the bottom of the fold together. Allow the children to work with partners, so one child can help pinch the bottom together while the other folds, and to help with dispensing the tape. **Make the part you've already folded curve, forming a circle.** (The bottom of the strip will become the inside of the circle.) **After you're done folding, use a small piece of tape to connect the ends, completing the circle. Then bring the folds together in the middle, pinching and bunching the folds until it looks even; tape the center back to keep the folds together.** (There will no longer be space in the center of the circle; all the inside edges are together.)

Cut your small piece of crepe paper into two pieces, and tape them to the back of the rosette, as ribbons hanging down the bottom of the rosette. Curl the edges by rolling them, if desired. Then take a loop of tape and secure the cardstock circle to the center of the rosette. Repeat to create other ribbons, as time allows. Display the completed ribbons under the heading, "God is . . . "

4 Closing (5 minutes)

To Prepare: Students need their Lesson 3 ticket. Gather in the worship area.

Sing "Silver and Gold" (*AGPS* 212:1), "Children of the Heavenly Father" (*LSB* 725; Director CD 1), or "We Praise You, O God" (*LSB* 785; Director CD 11).

Bring out your Lesson 3 fair ticket.

Say **Let's read today's theme: God is worthy of my thanks and praise. Look closely at the prize ribbon. What small numeral do you see on it?** (1) **If we were to give God a ribbon, why would we want to have a number one on it?** (There are no other gods besides our God. He desires and deserves our praise and the number one place in our lives.)

Say **As we pray our closing prayer, let's praise God with the words and qualities you chose for your blue ribbons to Him. As I begin the prayer, I'll say, "Dear God, You are . . ." Then I will stop and ask you to say the characteristic of God that you chose for your ribbon.**

Pray **Dear God, You are . . .** [qualities of God here]**. You and You alone are worthy of our thanks and praise. We thank You for Your care, protection, healing, love, and especially for the salvation and faith we receive from You for Jesus' sake. Give us joy-filled hearts so that we may praise You forever. In Jesus' name we pray. Amen.**

Direct the students to place their fair ticket into their prayer wheel pocket. As each person leaves, say, **God is worthy of our thanks and praise.**

Living the Faith

The Bible verse for this lesson is said by some Christians after they eat a meal. Say Psalm 136:1 after each meal you eat this week to thank our worthy God for the goodness, love, and mercy He gives us through all His gifts to us.

Snack

Blue-Ribbon Cake

Check with people in your congregation and see if anyone has ever baked a cake that won a ribbon in a food competition at a fair. Ask one or two of these individuals to bake the award-winning cake for your class. Or ask several bakers in your congregation to each make a small cake for your class. Let students sample each type of cake and choose a favorite. As a thank-you, give all bakers a ribbon or other small prize. (A healthier alternative is to sample clean, cut up "award-winning" garden produce.)

Our Champion God Is . . .

Directions: Find and read each Bible passage listed below. On the circular center of the award ribbon, write the descriptive name or quality of God the verse gives. Complete the sentence "Our champion God is ________________________" with one or two words.

Lesson 4

Preparing the Lesson

Jesus Teaches His Disciples to Pray

Luke 11:1–13—Jesus teaches me how to pray.

Key Point

Jesus taught His disciples and followers the Lord's Prayer to show them how to pray. God invites us to talk to Him using this same prayer today.

Law/**Gospel**

I am born in sin, cut off from God, unable to communicate with Him because of the barrier of sin. **Through Baptism and His Word, God creates faith in me, forgiving my sins for Jesus' sake and restoring my broken relationship with Him. He brings me into His family of faith and teaches me how to talk to Him.**

Context

Prior to this text, Jesus sent seventy-two disciples ahead of Him to all the cities where He was Himself about to go. They went out two by two to bring peace to the households that would receive them. Jesus told those He sent out, "The one who hears you hears Me, and the one who rejects you rejects Me, and the one who rejects Me rejects Him who sent Me" (Luke 10:16), indicating that believing in Jesus is what reconciles us with the Father. After the seventy-two returned, Jesus preached the parable of the Good Samaritan, in which He shows Himself as the neighbor to all people, coming to bind up their wounds, forgive their sins, and restore them to eternal life. In this context of Jesus' peace and mercy, He now teaches His disciples how to pray.

Commentary

It was common for religious teachers to instruct their students with regard to prayer and to give them set forms of prayer. John the Baptist taught his disciples how to pray (v. 1), but Scripture doesn't record the prayer for us. Jesus' disciples witnessed Him praying often. They knew this was His custom. He would withdraw to a desolate place and pray (Mark 1:35). Now, they wanted to be taught by their teacher how to pray.

Jesus gives His disciples the words to use for prayer. The words are important. They are from Jesus' own mouth. The Lord's Prayer is not only a set form of prayer but also a model for prayer. It is not a magical incantation, where if you say the right words in the right way, you can manipulate the divine. In fact, Matthew and Luke record the Lord's Prayer in slightly different forms. Matthew's version is longer than Luke's. Matthew follows the Lord's Prayer with a teaching about forgiving others their sins, but Luke follows with a teaching on making petition to God and not giving up.

The prayer that the Lord taught His disciples is broken up nicely into what we call petitions. A *petition* is a request. After the short introduction in Luke of the single form of address, "Father," he records Jesus giving five petitions: "Hallowed be Your name. Your kingdom come. Give us each day our daily bread. And forgive us our sins, for we ourselves forgive everyone who is indebted to us. And lead us not into temptation." He either omits two petitions that Matthew records or is simply recording another time when Jesus instructed His disciples on prayer. Both options are feasible.

After giving the words to the prayer, Jesus launches off into an analogy on praying with "impudence," that is, with boldness and audacity. A friend has the audacity to approach another friend in the middle of the night to ask for bread. Jesus teaches persistence and confidence in prayer. The Son promises that the Father will answer everyone who asks, seeks, and knocks. This is a confidence that only God can promise. Without this instruction, we may have otherwise been timid in our requests, thinking, *How dare I ask God for something?* However, Jesus encourages, even commands, us to ask and then follows it with a promise that the Father will hear and answer (v. 10).

Jesus' use of the word *father* in His analogy of how God hears our petitions is an expansion on the introduction of the Lord's Prayer. It's an analogy of the relationship that God has with those who believe in Jesus. God promises to give good things to His children. We are God's children by Baptism. And the chief good gift is the Holy Spirit, who grants life and salvation.

To hear an in-depth discussion of this Bible account, visit cph.org/podcast and listen to our Seeds of Faith podcast each week.

Lesson 4

Jesus Teaches His Disciples to Pray

Luke 11:1–13

Connections

Bible Words
Ask, and it will be given to you; seek, and you will find; knock, and it will be opened to you. Matthew 7:7

Faith Word
petition

Hymns and Songs
The King's Kids Are Prayin' (Director CD 9)

What a Friend We Have In Jesus (*LSB* 770; Director CD 13)

Knock, Knock (*AGPS* 152)

Children of the Heavenly Father (*LSB* 725; Director CD 1)

The Lord's Prayer (*AGPS* 173 or Director CD 10)

Catechism
Jesus gave us the Lord's Prayer [to show us how to pray]. (Question 204)

Take-Home Point
Jesus teaches me how to pray.

1 Opening (15 minutes)

Welcome

To Prepare: Before class, print the following on a poster and place outside of the door at the entrance to your classroom: *How to Pray*. Below these words, add the time your Sunday School begins (e.g., *9:00 a.m.*). Ideally, use two pieces of white poster board and attach one poster to each side of a freestanding easel, creating a two-sided signboard. Make copies of the Lesson 4 fair ticket (Director CD) and Resource Page 4, one per student. If possible, learn the American Sign Language signs for the words *ask*, *seek*, and *knock*. Provide copies of "A Responsive Reading on Prayer."

Sit behind the ticket window and greet students. Pass out Lesson 4 tickets.

Say **Welcome back to the Christian County Fair and to our Sunday School course, *Pray, Praise & Give Thanks: Jesus Teaches Us to Pray*. So far, we've explored several Bible accounts that have taught us some important truths about prayer. Today, we will begin to study the prayer that Jesus taught us, the Lord's Prayer. To begin, I'd like to demonstrate something about prayer.**

Demonstrate how to sign the words *ask*, *seek*, and *knock* in American Sign Language. Say the words as you make each sign. Sign each word several times. Then encourage the students to sign the words with you.

Web Activity: Locate or have students locate a video demonstration of the Lord's Prayer in sign language. Invite the students to try some of the signs along with the person on the video.

MATERIALS NEEDED

1 Opening	2 God Speaks	3 We Live	4 Closing
Director CD White poster board (1–2 sheets) Black permanent marker Two-sided freestanding signboard, easel, or sawhorse Masking tape Lesson 4 fair tickets (Director CD) Copies of "A Responsive Reading on Prayer" (Director CD or p. 12) Resource Page 4	Bibles Student Leaflet 4	Activity Page 4 White paper Highlighters or colored pencils Colored cardstock Drinking straws (25 per student) 15-inch length of ribbon or yarn (1 per student)	Director CD Lesson 4 fair tickets "How to Pray" sign (see Opening)

Say **I've just demonstrated in sign language three important words about prayer. At fairs, you'll see people demonstrating all kinds of different things. We'll find out more about that, but now let's begin our time at the fair with worship.** Move to the worship area of your classroom.

Worship

Sing "The King's Kids Are Prayin'" (Director CD 9) or "What a Friend We Have in Jesus" (*LSB* 770; Director CD 13). These songs introduce the Bible Words for this lesson as well as the encouragement Jesus gives us to pray.

Invocation **In the name of the Father and of the Son and of the Holy Spirit. Amen.**

Hand out copies of "A Responsive Reading on Prayer" (Director CD or p. 12).

Use the reading together.

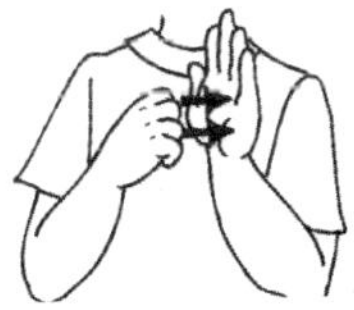

A "Fair"ly Good Clue to Learn a Fact about Prayer

Ask **Did you notice anything new or different as you entered the fair gate today?** (Bring the signboard you've prepared into the worship area.)

Say **At fairs, signboards like these are often used to direct people to special demonstrations that are scheduled throughout the day at various locations around the fairgrounds. Can you think of any demonstrations you've seen?** (Care for animals such as shearing sheep or milking cows, new kinds of farm products, new recipes and cooking products, etc.)

Ask **What does the poster say is going to be demonstrated at our fair today?** (How to pray)

Prayer at the Fair Opening Devotion

Ask **In the opening devotions for the first three lessons, we met a girl named Emily and her horse, Flash. At the fair so far, Emily has faced some challenges. In every difficulty or frustration, what has Emily demonstrated?** (How to pray to God, and also her trust in and dependence upon God for help and guidance)

Say **Let's find out about a special demonstration Emily is asked to do.**

Hand out Resource Page 4. Invite volunteers to take turns reading the story.

Ask **What kind of a demonstration did the judge ask Emily give to the other contestants?** (She showed them how to set up a horse for judging.)

Ask **What is the purpose of a demonstration?** (To teach someone the correct way to do something or to show how something works or can be used)

Direct students' attention once more to the "How to Pray" signboard.

Say **Today, we are going to study about a time when Jesus demonstrated for His disciples and for us how to pray.**

Offering Encourage the students as they give their offerings. Offerings give thanks to God for hearing our prayers.

Pray **Jesus, when we read and study Your Word, You teach us so many truths. As we study how You taught Your disciples and followers how to pray, help us to follow Your example. In Your name we pray. Amen.**

Celebrate Recognize student birthdays, Baptism birthdays, and significant family events in your routine manner.

2 God Speaks (20 minutes)

God Teaches about Prayer

To Prepare: Have Bibles, pencils, and Student Leaflet 4 ready for use.

Direct the students to be seated in the Blue-Ribbon Bible Stories arena. Help them to locate Luke 11:1–13. Invite a volunteer to read Luke 11:1 out loud.

Say **In Bible times, religious teachers taught their students about prayer and gave them words to pray. The first verse of this Bible account tells us that John the Baptist taught his followers to pray.**

Ask **According to Luke 11:1, what did the disciples see Jesus do?** (Pray) **What did one of the disciples request?** (For Jesus to teach them to pray)

Say **Let's read out loud together Luke 11:2–4.**

Direct the students to stand and read these verses in unison.

Ask **What's another name for what was read out loud?** (The Lord's Prayer)

Direct the students to turn to Luke 11:5.

Say **After Jesus demonstrated for the disciples how to pray, He carefully explained to them some very important information about prayer.**

Ask one volunteer to read Luke 11:5–8 out loud.

Ask **In verses 5–8, Jesus uses a short parable to teach about the way God answers our prayers. He told a story to teach us a lesson about prayer. How does the man in Jesus' parable answer his friend's request for bread?** (Although it was late and getting up would likely wake up his entire family, the man got out of bed and gave his friend what he needed.)

Ask **The man who gives the bread to his friend represents how God acts toward us when we pray to Him. How?** (The man listened to his friend's request for help. God listens to our prayers for help. The man gave his friend the bread he needed. God gives us what we need, according to His will.) **The man who asks for bread represents us. Jesus is teaching us how we should act toward God. The Bible uses the word *impudence*** (v. 8) **to describe how the man acted. That means the man was bold. How?** (He was persistent in his requests for help. He wasn't afraid to ask a favor even when it was in the middle of the night.) **What does this tell us about what we should do?** (Be bold/persistent in prayer; ask God anything, anytime.)

Ask a second volunteer to read verses 9–13 out loud.

Ask **How do verses 9–13 give even more proof of God's goodness toward us?** (Jesus *tells* us that God wants us to ask and to keep on asking Him for what we need. God promises to answer our requests in the best way for us.)

Ask a volunteer to reread out loud verse 13.

Ask **What good gift does our heavenly Father give to us, His children?** (The Holy Spirit) **God loves to give His children good gifts. He knows what we need. Why is the Holy Spirit so important?** (He gives us faith in the triune God, through whom we have forgiveness of sins and eternal life! The Holy Spirit works through God's Word and the Sacraments so we

Teacher Tip

Matthew 6:9–13 records another, longer version of the Lord's Prayer. In the Gospels (Matthew, Mark, Luke, and John), many of the same events are recorded. Some Gospel writers offer a longer or more complete version of the same event. Some students may ask why neither Matthew nor Luke include the conclusion of the Lord's Prayer. It is possible that later copyists of the Bible added it to the Matthew text; from the early days of the Christian Church it's been used. This conclusion to the prayer is a doxology, a statement that gives glory to God, so it was likely a later addition growing out of ancient liturgical use of the Lord's Prayer in Christian worship.

believe that Jesus is our Savior. He is at work our entire lives so that our faith grows.)

Review

Hand out Student Leaflet 4 and pencils. Encourage the students to work in pairs to unscramble the words in the Search & Know activity on page 4 to review the lesson details. **Answers:** 1. teach; 2. hallowed; 3. kingdom, bread, forgive; 4. temptation; 5. parable, friends; 6. Ask, seek, knock; 7. Holy Spirit.

Bible Words

Ask, and it will be given to you; seek, and you will find; knock, and it will be opened to you. Matthew 7:7

Locate the Bible Words on the student leaflet. Read them out loud together.

Say **In this Bible verse, Jesus tells us to keep on praying to God and to trust that God will hear and answer our prayers. Earlier today, we learned the signs for the words *ask*, *seek*, and *knock*. Let's review them.**

Demonstrate the signs once again using the diagrams found in the Opening section of this lesson. Let the students practice each sign with you several times. Then teach the three phrases of the verse using the signs.

3 We Live (20 minutes)

Pray, Praise & Give Thanks

To Prepare: Make copies of Activity Page 4 on white paper; cut in half. Have yellow, pink, and green highlighters or colored pencils ready for use, one set of three for every two students.

Ask **In our devotion earlier, what did Emily demonstrate?** (How to properly square up a horse for judging) **Why do you think the judge asked Emily to make this demonstration?** (Many of the other contestants did not know how to do this correctly. They needed someone to show them how.)

Ask **Do you sometimes find it hard to pray?** (Let students respond.) **What are some things that can make it hard for us to talk to God in prayer?** (We may not know how to begin. We may be distracted by noise around us. We may have trouble focusing our thoughts. We may have doubts that God actually hears us or cares about our needs. We may feel so guilty about something we have done that we feel we can't talk to God.)

Say **Our sins, our doubts, and our lack of knowledge are barriers to prayer. We may feel like we don't dare approach God because He's so holy and we're so sinful. But through Baptism and His Word, God makes us His children. He forgives our sins for Jesus' sake and invites us to talk to Him. In fact, He commands it! He promises to hear us and answer us.**

Hand out copies of Activity Page 4.

Say **So that we would know how to talk to God our Father in prayer, Jesus modeled, or demonstrated, a prayer for us that has come to be known as the Lord's Prayer. Let's read it out loud together.** Do so.

Ask **The words of this prayer may be very familiar to you. What are things you noticed about this prayer as you read it just now?** (The prayer is well organized; the beginning of the prayer is a bit like the way we begin a letter; the first three parts of the prayer after the beginning line are requests for spiritual blessings, then there is a request for material blessings, and then come requests to help us fight against sin and evil; etc.) Write the students' observations on the board, along with the Faith Word, *petition*.

Say **In the Lord's Prayer, Jesus gave us a perfect way to organize our thoughts as we talk to God in prayer. The first line of the prayer is an introduction to the prayer. The seven lines that follow are called petitions. A *petition* is a request, something for which we ask God. The last line of the prayer is its conclusion, giving God the glory He deserves. In the coming weeks, we will look carefully at each section of the Lord's Prayer. Right now, let's take a brief look at the seven petitions.**

Instruct the children to use a yellow highlighter or pencil to trace over the first three petitions on Activity Page 4: "Hallowed be Thy name"; "Thy kingdom come"; and "Thy will be done on earth as it is in heaven." Demonstrate.

Point to each petition on your copy of the Lord's Prayer as you talk about it.

Say **The first three petitions of the prayer are requests to God for spiritual blessings. In the First Petition, we pray that God's name be used respectfully and that God's Word be taught and used truthfully. In the Second Petition, we pray that God would help us live as His children in His kingdom here on earth and that He would bring others into faith in Him as their Savior. In the Third Petition, we pray that God's will be done among us as He breaks the hold of sin and Satan on us. We ask God to strengthen our faith and to keep growing our faith in Him.**

Instruct the children to use a pink highlighter or pencil to highlight the Fourth Petition, "Give us this day our daily bread," on Activity Page 4. Model.

Say **In the Fourth Petition, we pray that God would meet our physical needs. What are some of the physical needs we have?** (Food, clothing, homes, money, family, good government, health, friends, good weather, etc.)

Instruct the students to use a green highlighter or pencil to trace over the last three petitions on Activity Page 4. Demonstrate.

Say **The last three petitions of the Lord's Prayer are requests to God for deliverance from evil. In the Fifth Petition, we ask God to forgive us our sins and to help us to forgive those who sin against us. In the Sixth Petition, we ask God to guard and keep us from sinful thoughts and actions. In the Seventh Petition, we ask God to rescue us from all evil here on earth and to someday take us to heaven to live with Him.**

Ask **Why is it so important to pray boldly for deliverance from evil?** (Daily we struggle with temptations, sinful thoughts, words, and actions, with all kinds of evil that our sinful natures and Satan use to attack us and our faith. Our sins lead us to take our eyes off the cross of Christ and the truth that Jesus saved us from our sins. We need God's help every day so that we trust in Him alone and in the salvation that He gives us through Jesus.)

Have the students fold Activity Page 4 in half vertically and place it in their prayer wheel pocket in the worship area for use in future lessons.

Craft—Lord's Prayer Plaques

To Prepare: Make copies of Activity Page 4 on colored cardstock; cut each page in half. Cut a 15-inch length of ribbon or yarn for each student. Provide 20–25 colorful (or even striped or patterned) plastic drinking straws per student (bendy straws will work), transparent tape, scissors, and glue.

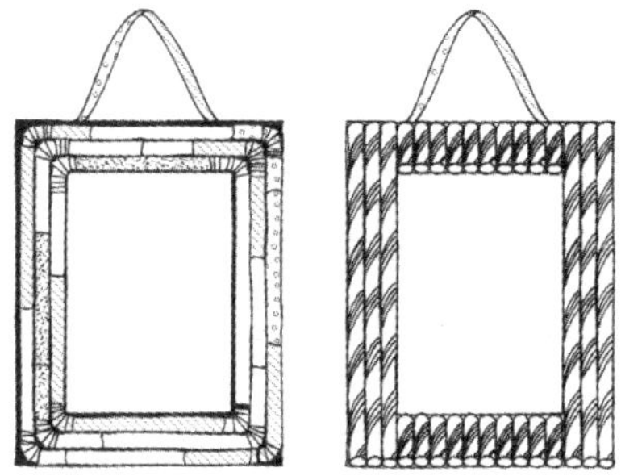

Hand out a trimmed copy of Activity Page 4 to each student.

Say **Let's make a Lord's Prayer plaque to hang somewhere at home to use as you pray to God. To give this plaque some "fair flair," let's make a frame for it using straws. Cut the straws in various lengths, and then glue them to the background paper around the words of the Lord's Prayer to frame them. Try not to cover any words of the prayer.**

Before the students begin to make the frame, give each person a piece of ribbon. Have them attach each end of the ribbon with tape to the back of the cardstock paper to make a hanger at the top. Then hand out the straws, scissors, and glue. Encourage students to be creative in the ways they cut and arrange their straws as they make their frames (e.g., extending some or all of the straws over the edge of the cardstock, placing straws haphazardly and overlapping, inserting the straw pieces one into another to form a continuous frame and repeating to make a wider border, lining up smaller straw pieces side by side). Students can cut off the bendy part of each straw or use the elbow pieces to form the corners of the frame.

Snack

Prayer Pretzels

At many fairs, hot soft pretzels are popular snacks. Purchase frozen pretzels and prepare according to package directions in an oven or microwave. As an option, purchase a bag of large twist pretzels (the hard, crunchy kind). Have the children turn their pretzel upside down and observe how the two ends of the pretzel overlap. Tradition says that pretzels were first made like this to imitate the way people would cross their arms over their chests when they prayed.

4 Closing (5 minutes)

To Prepare: Have a lesson ticket ready. Set the signboard in the worship area.

Sing "Knock, Knock" (*AGPS* 152) to review the Bible Words. Teach "Lord's Prayer" (*AGPS* 173:1) or "The Lord's Prayer" (Director CD 10).

Stand next to the "How to Pray" signboard. Look at the Lesson 4 fair tickets.

Ask **Why is a signboard a good symbol for today's lesson?** (They are used at fairs to inform fairgoers of demonstrations that are going on at the fair. In today's Bible story, Jesus demonstrated to His disciples how to pray. Jesus gave us the Lord's Prayer so that we have a model for talking to God.)

Say **Starting today and in each of our coming lessons, we will end our closing prayer by praying together the Lord's Prayer.**

Pray **Heavenly Father, we thank You for sending Your only Son, Jesus, to die and rise again so that we are no longer separated from You by sin and we are now able to come to You in prayer. We thank You, Jesus, for saving us and for teaching us how to pray. We now pray together the prayer that You taught us.** Pray the Lord's Prayer out loud together.

Direct the students to place their Lesson 4 fair ticket into their prayer wheel pocket. As each person leaves, say, **Jesus teaches us how to pray.**

Living the Faith

Encourage students to hang their Lord's Prayer plaques in a prominent place at home. In addition to regular family prayers, challenge them to pray the Lord's Prayer at the end of daily family devotions or other prayers.

The Lord's Prayer

Our Father who art in heaven,
hallowed be Thy name,
Thy kingdom come,
Thy will be done on earth as it is in heaven;
give us this day our daily bread;
and forgive us our trespasses
as we forgive those who trespass against us;
and lead us not into temptation,
but deliver us from evil.
For Thine is the kingdom and the power and the glory
forever and ever. Amen.

The Lord's Prayer

Our Father who art in heaven,
hallowed be Thy name,
Thy kingdom come,
Thy will be done on earth as it is in heaven;
give us this day our daily bread;
and forgive us our trespasses
as we forgive those who trespass against us;
and lead us not into temptation,
but deliver us from evil.
For Thine is the kingdom and the power and the glory
forever and ever. Amen.

Lesson 5

Preparing the Lesson

The Baptism of Jesus

Luke 3:15–22—God wants me to pray to Him.

Key Point

At Jesus' Baptism, God the Father said Jesus was His beloved Son. God, our Father in heaven, who has made us His children through water and the Word, invites us to come to Him without fear and to ask for anything.

Law/**Gospel**

My sinful flesh must be commanded to pray. The Second Commandment exhorts me to prayer because if it did not, I would despise prayer, let it fall out of use, and would think that only other people should pray. **Through water and the Word, God calls me to be His own dear child. He promises to hear all my prayers and to answer them for the sake of His Son, Jesus, who took my sins to the cross and gives me His righteousness.**

Context

Jesus is ready to begin His public ministry. John the Baptist is preparing His way by preaching of repentance, Baptism, and the forgiveness of sins. Luke provides references to the historical date, stating that it was in the fifteenth year of Tiberius Caesar, that Pontius Pilate was governor of Judea, and that the high priests were Annas and Caiaphas.

Everyone was coming out to hear John preach, and many were being baptized by him. The crowds, including tax collectors and soldiers, were learning how to live their lives in conformity to the coming of the Messiah (Hebrew for *Christ*). No one could use the excuse that they were Abraham's children. Everyone must repent and bear fruit.

Commentary

In their expectation, the people who listened to John and were baptized wondered if he was the Christ. But John clearly taught them that he was the forerunner. He told them that the Christ would come after him and be mightier than he was. John's Baptism granted forgiveness and entrance into the kingdom of heaven to those who repented of their sins (John 3:1–8). He baptized with water, but the Christ would baptize with the Holy Spirit and with fire.

After John baptized Jesus, the Holy Spirit descended in the form of a dove and rested upon Him (Luke 3:22; John 1:33). Then the Father spoke from heaven, "You are My beloved Son; with You I am well pleased" (v. 22). The clear reference to all three persons of the Trinity is important here. Baptism is a trinitarian event. God is present in the water according to all three persons.

The Baptism of Jesus is different from our Baptism. He is the sinless Son of God. He did not need to be baptized for the forgiveness of sins. He was baptized to take on our sins. Baptism washes us clean because Jesus bore our sins to the cross. That's why it was necessary for Jesus to be baptized at the beginning of His earthly ministry. It is the inauguration of our salvation. He is our substitute. He takes our sins and gives us His righteousness. He bears the condemnation of our sin and gives us His heavenly inheritance. In Baptism, we are made God's children. At each Christian Baptism, the heavens really are opened, the Spirit really descends upon the person, and the Father really adopts that person as His beloved child. From the time of our Baptism, we are God's children. We have received adoption as sons and daughters. We can rightly cry out, "Abba! Father!" And if we are children, then we are also heirs with Christ (Romans 8:14–17).

In the introduction to the Lord's Prayer, we confess that we are baptized into His family as His true children, and that He is our true Father. The relationship that He initiated with us in Baptism is the basis of our prayer and the confidence of our faith. The fact that we use the first person plural pronoun "our" places us into a community of the redeemed. We are never alone, even if we pray the Lord's Prayer by ourselves.

To hear an in-depth discussion of this Bible account, visit cph.org/podcast and listen to our Seeds of Faith podcast each week.

Lesson 5

The Baptism of Jesus

Luke 3:15–22

Connections

Bible Words
See what kind of love the Father has given to us, that we should be called children of God. 1 John 3:1

Faith Words
children of God

Hymns and Songs
The Lord's Prayer (*AGPS* 173 or Director CD 10)

Our Father, Who from Heaven Above (*LSB* 766; Director CD 7)

Come, My Soul, with Every Care (*LSB* 779; Director CD 2)

Catechism
The Introduction

The word *Father* tells us that God loves us and wants us to pray to Him confidently and without fear. (Question 205)

Take-Home Point
God wants me to pray to Him.

1 Opening (15 minutes)

Welcome

To Prepare: You will need a cell phone. Make copies of the Lesson 5 fair ticket (Director CD) and Resource Page 5, one per student. Have copies of "A Responsive Reading on Prayer" ready for use again today.

Sit behind the ticket window and greet students. Pass out Lesson 5 tickets.

Say **Welcome back to the Christian County Fair and to our Sunday School course, *Pray, Praise & Give Thanks: Jesus Teaches Us to Pray*. Today, we will continue our study of the prayer Jesus taught us, the Lord's Prayer.**

Bring out the cell phone.

Say **At fairs, people love to take pictures of family and friends. Let's use this cell phone to take some pictures of one another here at our fair.**

Invite students to pose in small groups around each area of the classroom "fairgrounds." Then gather the students back together and show the photos.

Say **Cell phones are a way to share fun times and to communicate information with others, especially with family members. Today, we will find out more about communicating with our Father . . . in heaven. Let's start by singing and praying to Him.** Move to the worship area.

Worship

Sing "Come, My Soul, with Every Care" (*LSB* 779; Director CD 2). We pray to and worship God!

MATERIALS NEEDED

1 Opening	2 God Speaks	3 We Live	4 Closing
Director CD Cell phone that can take pictures Lesson 5 fair tickets (Director CD) Copies of "A Responsive Reading on Prayer" (Director CD or p. 12) Resource Page 5	Bibles Student Leaflet 5 Copies of rhyming story Poster board or butcher paper	Bibles Activity Page 5 Thin dowel rods, at least 1 per child White cardstock Cell phone	Director CD Lesson 5 fair tickets Cell phone

Invocation **In the name of the Father and of the Son and of the Holy Spirit. Amen.**

Hand out copies of "A Responsive Reading on Prayer" (Director CD or p. 12). Use the reading together.

A "Fair"ly Good Clue to Learn a Fact about Prayer

Ask **What symbol do you see on today's ticket?** (Cell phone) **Imagine you are with your family at the fair. How might you use a cell phone while you are there?** (Let a parent know where you are on the fair grounds and that you are safe, send a text message about a time and place where to meet to get something to eat or to see a fair event, take and send photos)

Ask **How might a cell phone be a "fair"ly good clue to learn a fact about prayer?** (It is a way to communicate. In prayer we communicate with God.)

Prayer at the Fair Opening Devotion

Hand out Resource Page 5.

Say **After her blue-ribbon win at the horse show, Emily and her dad spent some time together at the fair. Let's find out what they did.**

Invite volunteers to take turns reading out loud the story.

Ask **How did Emily and her dad use a cell phone as they rode the Ferris wheel?** (They took a "selfie" photo of themselves. They also received a text message from Emily's mom about where to meet her.)

Ask **How would you describe the relationship between Emily and her father?** (They love each other. Emily's dad is proud of her. He loves to teach her. Emily loves to spend time with her dad.)

Ask **Why do you think Emily and her father have a strong and loving relationship?** (They communicate with each other and spend time together. God has blessed their relationship.)

Ask **All of us have a Father in heaven: God. Today, we will find out how we become a part of God's family and how God wants us to pray to Him. We'll see how prayer is an important part of our relationship with Him.**

Offering Encourage the students as they give their offerings. Offerings give thanks to our heavenly Father for His love.

Pray **Heavenly Father, thank You for this day. Bless our time together now, as we find out more about You and Your love for Your children, as we study Your Word. Thank You for promising to hear and answer us for Jesus' sake. In His name we pray. Amen.**

Celebrate Recognize student birthdays, Baptism birthdays, and significant family events in your routine manner.

Web Activity: Locate information about the Ferris wheel and the man who invented it, George Washington Gale Ferris Jr. Relate this information to today's devotion as well as to the prayer wheel in your classroom worship area. Marvel how we can be at the top of a Ferris wheel and see everything at the fair. Remind the children that God sees everything and knows what we need.

Teacher Tip

Before taking pictures of your students, be sure to get permission from parents or guardians.

2 God Speaks (20 minutes)

God Teaches about Prayer

To Prepare: Have Bibles ready for use. Make a copy of "The Baptism of Jesus" rhyming story from this section. Cut the story into three parts as indicated by the spaces between sections in the story. Provide three large sheets of poster board or butcher paper, markers, and pencils. Have Student Leaflet 5 ready.

Hand out Bibles and help students locate Luke 3:15–22. Read verses 15–18.

Ask **What do these verses tell you about John the Baptist?** (He denied that he was the Messiah. John explained that someone much greater than he was coming, who would baptize them with the Holy Spirit and with fire, giving them faith and eternal life.) **What else did John do?** (He preached good news to the people that the Savior was coming.)

Read out loud verses 19–20.

Ask **What did Herod eventually do to John?** (He put John in prison because he had reproved, or sternly told, Herod that he was wrong for marrying Herodias, the wife of his brother, and for other evil things he had done. Eventually, John was killed due to Herodias's evil scheming [Mark 6:14–29].)

Say **After the Gospel writer Luke tells about John the Baptist's life, he gives us a flashback to an event that happened earlier, when John was baptizing people at the Jordan River.**

Read out loud verses 21–22.

Say **Jesus came to John to be baptized, but not because He was sinful. Jesus was baptized to give us His righteousness** (holiness)**. Later, Jesus died for all the sins of all people. He took our sins and the punishment for our sins upon Himself when He was crucified.**

Ask **After Jesus was baptized by John, what did He do?** (Prayed to God. Jesus modeled the importance of communicating with our heavenly Father.) **What happened next?** (The heavens opened, and Jesus saw the Holy Spirit, in the form of a dove, descend and rest upon Him. Then God the Father said to Jesus, "You are My beloved Son; with You I am well pleased.")

Divide the students into three groups. To review, use the rhyming action story. After each couplet, have the students repeat the words and the action with you, or let the students each do their own action for the couplet.

John the Baptist followed God,
Cleared the way for Christ to trod, — *Walk in place.*

Told the people to repent.
At the Jordan, time John spent, — *Point and shake index finger.*

Used the water to baptize,
Helped his followers realize — *Cup hand, pretend to pour water.*

Jesus Christ was coming soon.
He would save from sin and doom. — *Form cross with index fingers.*

John told all, "Soon you will see
Someone who is greater than me." — *Bow head.*

One day on the Jordan's shore, **John was there, just as before.**	*Stand still.*
Jesus came there to fulfill **God His heav'nly Father's will.**	*Gesture upward with hand.*
Jesus said, "John, baptize me." **John replied, "I'm not worthy."**	*Shake head "no."*
But John did what Jesus said. **John poured water on His head.**	*Cup hand, pretend to pour water.*
Now baptized, Lord Jesus prayed, **To His Father, that blessed day.**	*Stand still, bow head, fold hands.*
Then the heavens opened wide. **Down from heav'n a dove did glide:**	*Flutter fingers of right hand in air.*
God the Spirit for God's Son. **Jesus' work on earth's begun!**	*Point up to heaven, then down.*
Then the Father Himself spoke, **Wanted everyone to note:**	*Raise arms upward, look up.*
"This is My beloved Son **Who pleases Me with what He's done."**	*Nod head yes and smile.*

Give each group a sheet of poster board or paper, markers, pencils, and one section of the rhyming story you have copied and cut apart.

Say **Reread the part of the rhyming story that you've just been given. Draw a picture on the poster board to illustrate your part of the story.**

Encourage the students in each group to work together on their illustration. When the groups are finished, have several group members hold up their poster while other group members take turns reading the story section.

Review

Hand out Student Leaflet 5. Work together as a class or in partners to complete the Search & Know activity on page 4. Direct the students to look back at the Bible account if they are unsure of how to correct a sentence. As the students complete them, print the corrected words (or sentences) on the board. **Answers:** 1. mightier; 2. the Holy Spirit and fire; 3. Good News; 4. prayed; 5. heavens; 6. The Holy Spirit, dove; 7. well pleased.

Bible Words

See what kind of love the Father has given to us, that we should be called children of God. 1 John 3:1

Locate the Bible Words on the student leaflet. Read them out loud together. Write the Faith Words, *children of God*, on the board.

Ask **How do we become God's children?** (Through Baptism) **Through water and the Word, we are given faith and we become a part of God's family. When we are baptized, God, our Father in heaven, gives us many wonderful blessings. One blessing is that He invites us to come to Him without fear and to ask Him for anything. And as children, we receive our inheritance—a home in heaven with our Father, forever!**

Read together the Bible Words several times from the student leaflet.

3 We Live (20 minutes)

Pray, Praise & Give Thanks

To Prepare: Make copies of Activity Page 5. Provide pencils. Have students get their copy of the Lord's Prayer (Activity Page 4) from their prayer wheel pocket. Have some extra copies of the prayer on hand for those without one.

Ask **What did God call Jesus after He was baptized?** (His "beloved Son") **Because Jesus is God's Son, what does Jesus call God?** (His Father)

Ask **Look at your copy of the Lord's Prayer. Where in the prayer does Jesus use the words "Our Father"?** (At the very beginning of the prayer when He prays, "Our Father, who art in heaven." These words are known as the Introduction to the Lord's Prayer.) Point to the Faith Words, *children of God*, that you previously printed on the board.

Ask **Our Bible Words for this lesson said that we are "children of God." What does this allow us to call God?** (Through Baptism, we are God's children; therefore, we can call God our Father, as Jesus does.)

Ask **Communication is the way family members stay connected. How do we communicate with God, our heavenly Father?** (Prayer) **God wants us to pray to Him. He is the best and perfect Father who has created us and continues to love us always, so He wants to have a relationship with us. When we are baptized, we become a part of God's family. We are now children of God. As His children, God invites us to pray to Him.**

The Bible tells us more about this wonderful relationship we have with God, our Father in heaven. Let's explore this now.

Hand out Activity Page 5. Ask a volunteer to read out loud the directions on the page. Work together as a class to crack the coded words in each Bible verse and to answer the questions about our relationship with God, using the information found in each verse. Remind the students that grace is the undeserved love and blessings which we receive from God through faith in Jesus.

Answers:

1. What is our relationship to God? (God is our Father, and we are His sons and daughters.) 2 Corinthians 6:18: *father; sons; daughters*
2. Because God is our Father, how does He want us to pray to Him? (With confidence) Because God is our Father, what will we receive when we pray to Him? (Mercy and grace, for Jesus' sake) Hebrews 4:16: *confidence; mercy; grace*
3. How do we become God's children? (Through faith in Jesus) Galatians 3:26: *Christ Jesus; faith*
4. What do the words of the Lord's Prayer, "Our Father who art in heaven," say about God? (He is Lord over all, so He has the power to grant our prayers.) Psalm 124:8: *help; LORD; heaven; earth*

At the end of this part of the lesson, have the students place their copies of the Lord's Prayer (Activity Page 4) back into their prayer wheel pocket.

Craft—Child of God "Selfie" Props

To Prepare: Provide white cardstock, thin wooden dowels, markers, pencils, scissors, and masking tape. Bring your phone. Search online for free printable photo booth props (especially crowns, thought and speech bubbles, and expressive eyes and mouths to show emotions that might motivate a child to talk to God, such as joy, sorrow, fear, or grief). Download the images and print them onto cardstock. Write short, prayerful phrases on the speech bubbles, such as "Thank You, God!" "Help!" "I'm sorry," and "Forgive me."

Say **Let's make some photo booth props to hold in front of us while we take selfies to remind us that we can talk to our heavenly Father.**

Hand out the preprinted props for students to cut out, or show them examples of photo booth props and give them time to create their own eyes, mouths, speech bubbles, or crowns. Securely tape the dowels to one side of the back of the prop; alternate left or right, so they're not all the same.

Say **Let's take some selfies of you praying to God! Find two props to hold up to your face and create a story you can tell with your picture. By your pose, I should be able to tell if you're thanking or praising God, telling Him you're sorry, asking Him a request, or calling upon Him in trouble.**

Use your camera to take a picture of each child, one at a time. Children may also want to work with a partner to expand the story line. Have students practice their poses and storytelling while waiting for their turn.

Snack

Snow Cones

Snow cones are popular fair treats. Make your own by placing crushed ice into paper cones or 5-ounce paper cups. Slowly pour purchased snow cone flavorings or prepared presweetened powdered drink mix flavors over the ice. Serve with drinking straws and spoons for a cool treat. Ice, of course, is frozen water. Talk about how the water of Holy Baptism combined with God's Word cleanses the sin from our hearts and makes us God's children, who can freely come to their heavenly Father in prayer for Jesus' sake.

4 Closing (5 minutes)

To Prepare: Have your Lesson 5 fair ticket ready for use and your cell phone.

Sing "Lord's Prayer" (*AGPS* 173:1–2), "The Lord's Prayer" (Director CD 10), or "Our Father, Who from Heaven Above" (*LSB* 779:1; Director CD 7).

Bring your cell phone. Have the students bring out their Lesson 5 tickets.

Ask **What is today's "fair"ly good clue about prayer?** (A cell phone)

Ask **Of what fact about prayer does the cell phone symbol remind us?** (The cell phone symbol reminds us that God wants us to pray to Him. As His loved children, God our heavenly Father invites us to talk to Him in prayer.)

Pray **Dear heavenly Father, we thank You for making us Your children through Holy Baptism. Through faith, we know that you want us to pray to You and that You have the power to hear and to answer our prayers. And now we pray together the prayer that Jesus taught us to pray.** Conclude by praying the Lord's Prayer out loud together.

Direct the students to place their Lesson 5 fair ticket into their prayer wheel passenger pocket. As each person leaves, say, **God wants us to pray to Him.**

Living the Faith

Encourage the students throughout the week to thank God in prayer for the Means of Grace He gives in Holy Baptism. In Holy Baptism, we become a part of God's family, a child of the heavenly King. What a marvelous gift!

Our Father Who Art in Heaven

Directions: Parts of each Bible verse below are written in code based on the keys on this cell phone. Match each symbol to its corresponding letter on the cell phone keyboard to find out more about what it means when we pray, "Our Father who art in heaven."

2 Corinthians 6:18: And I will be a 5 % 3 / 1 2 to you, and you shall be * (' * and 4 % - 6 / 3 1 2 * to Me, says the Lord Almighty.
_ _ _ _ _ _   _ _ _ _   _ _ _ _ _ _ _ _ _ _

What is our relationship to God? ______________________________

Hebrews 4:16: Let us then with 7 (' 5 _ 4 1 ' 7 1 draw near to the throne of grace, that we may
_ _ _ _ _ _ _ _ _ _

receive " 1 2 7 + and find 6 2 % 7 1 to help in time of need.
_ _ _ _ _   _ _ _ _ _

Because God is our Father, how does He want us to pray to Him? ______________________________

Because God is our Father, what will we receive when we pray to Him? ______________________________

Galatians 3:26: For in 7 / 2 _ * 3 : 1 * - * you are all sons of God, through 5 % _ 3 / .
_ _ _ _ _ _ _   _ _ _ _ _   _ _ _ _ _

How do we become God's children? ______________________________

Psalm 124:8: Our / 1 @) is in the name of the @ (2 4 , who made / 1 % 8 1 ' and 1 % 2 3 / .
_ _ _ _   _ _ _ _   _ _ _ _ _ _ _   _ _ _ _ _

What do the words of the Lord's Prayer, "Our Father who art in heaven," say about God?

____

Lesson 6

Preparing the Lesson

Zacchaeus

Luke 19:1–10—God helps me keep His name holy.

Key Point

Zacchaeus joyfully responded to His Savior's invitation, showing the Word of God at work in him. We keep God's name holy and glorify Him as we live according to His Word, letting His light shine through us.

Law/**Gospel**

I take what does not belong to me because I think that it will either help me or make me happy, but breaking God's Law always makes me miserable. **Jesus frees me from my misery through the forgiveness of sins. Thus freed, I am empowered by the Holy Spirit to live according to God's Word and bear fruits of repentance, not to earn forgiveness, but as a response to salvation.**

Context

Jesus is on His way up to Jerusalem. He just told His disciples for the third time that He must go to Jerusalem to fulfill all that the prophets foretold—to die and to rise again. He is passing through city after city teaching and working miracles. These are His final days before the triumphal entry into Jerusalem on Palm Sunday. Scripture records Jericho as His last stop before reaching Bethany, outside of Jerusalem.

As He was entering Jericho, He healed a blind beggar (Luke 18:42). While in Jericho, at Zacchaeus's house, Jesus told the people the parable about the ten minas (Luke 19:11–27). On His way out of town, He healed two blind men (Matthew 20:29–34), one of whom was Bartimaeus (Mark 10:46–52).

Commentary

Jericho was not Jesus' destination. He was only passing through. However, while He did, He worked at least two miracles, changed a man's life, and told a parable to the people. By an intentional visit to a tax collector's house, He demonstrated God's desire to save the lost.

Zacchaeus had heard about Jesus and desired to see Him. By this time, Jesus was so popular that people crowded around to see Him and to listen to His teachings. Many approached Him to receive healing. Zacchaeus, being too short to see over the crowds, ran ahead and climbed up in a tree near where Jesus would pass by.

Out of all the people who were around Him, Jesus sought out Zacchaeus for lodging that night. This request to stay at his house was a tremendous honor, and if Zacchaeus was not already motivated to repent and bear fruits of repentance, then he certainly became so upon Jesus' visit with him in his house.

Consider the disparaging reaction of the crowd to Zacchaeus's reaction to the request. Zacchaeus receives Jesus joyfully. The crowd grumbles. The crowd still does not understand that Jesus does not pay attention to what people expect of Him. He works for the lost, the miserable, the lonely, the poor, and the needy. Jesus is the Physician who comes to heal the sick. He is the Shepherd who searches out the lost sheep while leaving the ninety-nine.

Jesus' merciful action prompted Zacchaeus to repent of his sins and make restitution for his wrongs. Tax collectors were notorious thieves in first-century Judea. They were Jewish people under the service of the Roman government. Tax collectors were seen as traitors. The Romans used them to keep an accurate record of the people (Luke 2:1) and to collect money (Matthew 9:9). They were supposed to collect a certain amount for the Roman government, but if they collected more, then they got to keep it themselves. Everyone knew that they collected more than they were supposed to, but as the tax collectors were under the protection of the Roman army, no one could refuse to pay upon penalty of punishment. Eight times in the Gospels, the reproachful phrase "tax collectors and sinners" shows how negatively people thought of tax collectors.

After Zacchaeus's promise to give half of his wealth to the poor and to give back even more than he had stolen from the people, Jesus confirms what had happened to Zacchaeus's heart. He says that salvation has come to Zacchaeus, for Jesus came to seek and save the lost.

God's name is kept holy when His Word is taught in truth and purity and when children of God also live holy lives according to it. Faith and actions go hand in hand. When we believe that Jesus has forgiven our sins, our faith is seen in action and God's name is kept holy among us. But false teaching leads to living contrary to God's Word. We ask Him to protect us from this.

To hear an in-depth discussion of this Bible account, visit cph.org/podcast and listen to our Seeds of Faith podcast each week.

Lesson 6

Zacchaeus

Luke 19:1–10

Connections

Bible Words

Let your light shine before others, so that they may see your good works and give glory to your Father who is in heaven. Matthew 5:16

Faith Word

hallow

Hymns and Songs

We Come, O Lord, This Day (*AGPS* 253)

The Lord's Prayer (*AGPS* 173 or Director CD 10)

Our Father, Who from Heaven Above (*LSB* 766; Director CD 7)

Catechism

The First Petition

We keep God's name holy when God's Word is taught among us in its truth and purity [and] when we live according to the Word of God. (Question 210)

Take-Home Point

God helps me keep His name holy.

1 Opening (15 minutes)

Welcome

To Prepare: Make copies of the Lesson 6 fair ticket (Director CD), Resource Page 6, and "A Responsive Reading on Prayer" (Director CD), one per student.

Sit behind the ticket window and greet students. Pass out Lesson 6 tickets.

Say **Welcome back to the Christian County Fair and to our Sunday School course, *Pray, Praise & Give Thanks: Jesus Teaches Us to Pray.* Today, we will continue our study of the prayer Jesus taught us, the Lord's Prayer.**

Ask **If you wanted to participate in a county fair, what are some things that might be necessary to do?** (Make a project, learn a talent or skill, etc.)

Say **Most fairs require that each participant fill out an entry form and send it in weeks and even months before the fair begins. Sometimes some money also has to be sent in with the form to help pay fair expenses, judges' fees, and prize fees.**

Ask **What do you think is the most important fact to include on an entry form?** (Name of the participant or exhibitor) **On nearly every entry form, the name of the person participating is the first piece of information asked for. Without a name on an entry form, what happens?** (The person entering the activity is unknown.)

Say **Our name identifies who we are. God's name identifies who He is. Today, we will learn that God helps us keep His name holy. Let's continue with song and prayer.** Move to the worship area.

MATERIALS NEEDED

1 Opening	2 God Speaks	3 We Live	4 Closing
Director CD Lesson 6 fair tickets (Director CD) Copies of "A Responsive Reading on Prayer" (Director CD or p. 12) Resource Page 6	Bibles Student Leaflet 6 Flashlights, 1 per child (optional)	Activity Page 6 9 × 12-inch construction paper sheets, each cut into six 4-inch squares; 6 white squares, 3 colored squares per child 12 × 18-inch construction paper sheet, cut into 12-inch square, 1 per child	Director CD Lesson 6 fair tickets

Worship

Sing "We Come, O Lord, This Day" (*AGPS* 253) or "Our Father, Who from Heaven Above" (*LSB* 766:2; Director CD 7) to emphasize the importance of praying to and worshiping God.

Invocation **In the name of the Father and of the Son and of the Holy Spirit. Amen.**

Hand out copies of "A Responsive Reading on Prayer" (Director CD or p. 12).

Use the reading together.

A "Fair"ly Good Clue to Learn a Fact about Prayer

Invite the students to take out their Lesson 6 prayer ticket.

Ask **What symbol clue to do you see on today's ticket?** (Entry form) **Whose name do you see on the entry form?** (God's) **When you hear the name *God*, what thoughts come to your mind?** (Let the students share.)

Say **A few lessons ago, we made blue ribbons to honor God for all the great things He has done and continues to do for us. God is worthy of all of our praise and thanks. When we use God's name in praise to Him, we keep His name holy.**

Ask **How might this entry form with God's name be a "fair"ly good clue to learn about prayer?** (There is only one true God whom we worship. When we see God's name, we think of His greatness and of His love toward us. He is the only God we listen to, who guides us in the way we should live.)

Prayer at the Fair Opening Devotion

Hand out Resource Page 6.

Say **Let's find out about something special that happened at the fair queen contest.** Ask volunteers to take turns reading out loud the story.

Ask **How did Hannah, the outgoing fair queen, give glory to God?** (She praised God for the opportunity to serve as fair queen. She acknowledged that her strength to serve came from God. As she crowned the next queen, Hannah advised her to put God first.)

Say **God helps us to keep His name holy. In our Bible story, we will see how God's Word was at work in a man's life. Think about how faith in Jesus changed this man so that he kept God's name holy as he honored God with the way he lived, looking first to Him and to His will for us.**

Offering Encourage the students as they give. Giving to God in thanks is one of the ways we respond to salvation and live according to God's Word.

Pray **Most merciful God, You help us to keep Your name holy as we study Your Word. Bless our time together today, and open our hearts to see Your constant love for us. Help us to glorify You in all that we think, say, and do. In Jesus' name we pray. Amen.**

Celebrate Recognize student birthdays, Baptism birthdays, and significant family events in your routine manner.

Web Activity: Locate information about the various competitions in your county (or state) fair. Pray that those who participate would give glory to God as they compete.

2 God Speaks (20 minutes)

God Teaches about Prayer

To Prepare: Have Bibles, Student Leaflet 6, and pencils ready for use.

Direct the students to the Blue-Ribbon Bible stories arena. Hand out Bibles to each student and help them locate Luke 19:1–10. Assign the following roles: two narrators, Zacchaeus, Jesus, a tree (two students), the crowd, and a house (two students). Present this Bible account as a skit. Select two students to be narrators, one reading the odd-numbered verses and the other reading the even-numbered verses. They will read only verses and verse parts that do not have conversation in them; watch the use of quotation marks.

Say **This Bible account takes place as Jesus traveled to Jerusalem. While passing through Jericho, crowds had gathered to see Jesus.**

Narrator 1 reads verse 1: Crowd stands in two lines, facing each other, with a "road" in between them. They say, "We want to see Jesus."

Narrator 2 reads verse 2: Zacchaeus walks in, behind the crowd.

Narrator 1 reads verse 3: Jesus walks down road. Zacchaeus runs back and forth behind the crowd, jumping to see over the crowd.

Narrator 2 reads verse 4: Tree, at the end of the crowd, spreads out their arms as branches; Zacchaeus stands between (not on) them, climbing in place, then smiles when he "reaches the top."

Narrator 1 and Jesus read verse 5: Jesus stands in front the tree.

Narrator 2 reads verse 6: Zacchaeus climbs in place "down" the tree, smiling in joy, walks with Jesus down the "road."

Narrator 1 and crowd read verse 7: Crowd grumbles. Tree turns into a house (or use new actors); two children raise their arms to form a V-shaped "roof."

Narrator 2 and Zacchaeus read verse 8: Jesus and Zacchaeus stand under the "roof" of Zacchaeus's house.

Narrator 1 and Jesus read verses 9–10.

Option: Perform in Readers Theater style. Students stand in a semicircle and read and do all the actions (e.g., jumping, climbing) from that spot.

Review

Hand out Student Leaflet 6 and pencils. Let students work on this activity independently. Then review the correct answers together. **Answers:** climbed a tree: *Zacchaeus*; passed through Jericho: *Jesus*; grumbled: *crowd*; collected taxes: *Zacchaeus*; wanted to see Jesus: *Zacchaeus, crowd*; hosted dinner: *Zacchaeus*; stole money: *Zacchaeus*; came to seek and to save the lost: *Jesus*; gathered on the street: *crowd, Zacchaeus*; repented of sin: *Zacchaeus*; showed someone honor: *Zacchaeus*; was a sinner: *Zacchaeus, crowd*.

Teacher Tip

To simplify the task, students can write *J*, *Z*, or *C* on the blank line.

Bible Words

Let your light shine before others, so that they may see your good works and give glory to your Father who is in heaven. Matthew 5:16

Locate the Bible Words on the student leaflet. Read the verse together.

To Prepare: Provide small flashlights for each child (optional).

Ask **How was Hannah from our devotion a shining light?** (She gave thanks to God for blessing her and for helping her. As she did this, she gave God glory and hallowed His name. The crowd heard her words of praise to God and heard about her good works. They recognized the faith God gave her.)

Ask **Was Zacchaeus a shining light?** (Not always. At first, Zacchaeus used his job to steal from others. But when Jesus invited Himself into Zacchaeus's life, Jesus led him to repent of his sinful ways. God worked in Zacchaeus and helped him shine the light of faith as he gave half of his belongings to the poor and restored to others four times the amount he had taken.)

Ask **When God works in us as we praise Him, follow His Word, and keep His name holy, what do we show others?** (By the power of the Holy Spirit, when we follow God's will and look to God's Word to direct our lives, God works in us to show others His saving love. Through our good works, others will realize that God is the one who deserves our praise and honor.)

Divide the class into three groups. Have each group learn one-third of the verse: Let your light shine before others, / so that they may see your good works / and give glory to your Father who is in heaven.

Have everyone scramble away from their original group to a different area of the classroom and sit down. As you say the first word of the first part of the verse ("Let"), have the students who learned that part of the verse pop up and say the verse part with you, then quickly sit down. Continue in this manner with the other two parts of the verse, inviting students to pop up and down on their part of the verse. As an option, provide flashlights for each child and have the students turn them on when they stand and say their part, so that there are flashes of light going on and off throughout the verse.

3 We Live (20 minutes)

Pray, Praise & Give Thanks

To Prepare: Make copies of Activity Page 6. Provide pencils. Have students get their copy of the Lord's Prayer (Activity Page 4) from their prayer wheel pocket.

Have the students look at their copy of the Lord's Prayer.

Say **The First Petition, or request, that we make to our Father in heaven in the Lord's Prayer is "Hallowed be Thy name."**

Write the Faith Word, *hallow*, on the board.

Ask **The word *hallow* means "to make or keep holy." What does it mean when something is holy?** (Something or someone is good and pure. It is so special that it is set apart from other things that aren't good or pure.) **We hallow God's name, or keep it holy, when we live according to God's Word as it is taught to us in its truth and purity.**

Ask **On our own, is it easy to live according to God's Word? Is it easy to do God's will and follow His commands?** (No. On our own, it's impossible for us to live as God wants us to live.) **What are some things that can get**

in the way of keeping God's name holy in our lives? (Our own selfish, sinful natures and the temptations from Satan and from the world around us get in the way. We do what we think will make us happy, even if it means taking what doesn't belong to us or believing teachings that aren't true.) **As sinners, we don't want to follow God or honor God. We don't want to use His name to glorify Him. We want to do things our own way.**

Ask **What evidence do you see of this in Zacchaeus's life?** (Before Zacchaeus knew Jesus, he stole whatever he wanted from the people from whom he collected taxes. He became rich at the expense of others.)

Ask **What happened when Jesus invited Himself to Zacchaeus's house and into his life?** (By the power of the Holy Spirit, Zacchaeus came to know Jesus as His Savior. The Holy Spirit led Zacchaeus to recognize the sins he committed. Zacchaeus was joyful because Jesus forgave His sins.)

Ask **How do you know that Zacchaeus was sorry for his sins?** (He gave half of what he owned to the poor. He restored four times the money he had taken from people. This is also evidence of the light of Jesus' forgiveness and salvation shining in Zacchaeus's heart and soul and in his words and actions. Without God, Zacchaeus would never have done that!)

Say **Jesus came to find and save all sinners. He changes us so that we don't live life according to our own will, but according to God's will. Because of what our great God has done for us through Jesus, we want to keep His name holy. We want to be shining lights for God so that others may see how wonderful He is.**

Hand out Activity Page 6.

Say **In the livestock barns on this page are examples of people who are hallowing God's name as they live according to the Word of God by the power of the Holy Spirit working faith in their hearts.**

Read out loud the directions on the activity page. Work together as a class to match the Bible verses to the corresponding scene.

Suggested Activity Page answers: 1. C, Psalm 50:15; 2. B, Psalm 118:1; 3. A, 1 Chronicles 29:13; 4. D, Philippians 4:23. Note that more than one verse can fit a particular scene.

Ask **What are some particular things that God helps you to do to keep His name holy?** (Any activities in which students pray to God to praise and thank Him or ask for His help, anytime we recognize God and His work in our lives) **God works in us. Jesus changes us! In response to His forgiveness, we do good works, the result of the Holy Spirit at work in our lives.**

Return the Lord's Prayer copies back into the prayer wheel pockets.

Teacher Tip

If time permits, give the students time to color pictures that tell about God in the blank squares of the quilt. Or emphasize the fruit of the Spirit in our lives and have students draw four pictures showing how we can let our light shine, giving glory to God.

Craft—Glorifying God Quilt

To Prepare: Each child will need one 12 × 12-inch square of construction paper, six 4-inch squares of white construction paper, and three 4-inch squares of colored construction paper (ideally, yellow). Make the big square by trimming six inches from a 12 × 18-inch sheet. Trim 9 × 12-inch sheets to get 8 × 12-inch sheets; then cut each sheet into six 4-inch squares. Also provide crayons and glue sticks. Make an example to show, copy and enlarge the sample diagram, or show an example of an Ohio Star quilt block online.

Say **One of the most popular exhibits at many fairs are homemade quilts. Let's make a special quilt with a star pattern to remember to let our light shine so God will be glorified.**

Give a precut 12 × 12-inch square to each child. Explain that this is the base to which they will glue all other quilt pieces. Give each child four white squares and one colored square.

Say **Place four white blocks at each corner; we won't glue them yet. Then place a colored** (yellow) **square in the middle. With the remaining openings on our quilt, we will need to place smaller quilt pieces. But first, we need to cut them into triangle shapes.**

Give each child their two other colored squares. Show the students how to make the corners touch, creating a triangle, then repeat, making an even smaller triangle. Unfold and cut on the fold lines, creating four triangles from each square. Students should have eight colored triangles total.

Say **Look at the sample and place the colored triangles in the remaining spaces on your quilt in that way. Two squares have the triangles at the sides, and two squares have them top and bottom. Make the top tips of the triangles touch. Now repeat what you just did with white squares.**

Give each child their two other white squares. Repeat the folding to create four triangles each, and cut into eight total triangles. Students can place the final triangles in the remaining sections on the quilt.

Say **The star** (and images) **remind us of the greatness of our God—His glory—and remind us to give Him the glory by letting our light shine. Now glue the pieces into place. Take off one piece at a time, add glue to the back, then reposition in the same spot.**

4 Closing (5 minutes)

To Prepare: Have your Lesson 6 fair ticket ready for use.

Sing "Lord's Prayer" (*AGPS* 173:1–2, 5) or "The Lord's Prayer" (Director CD 10).

Have students bring out their Lesson 6 fair tickets.

Ask **What is today's "fair"ly good clue about prayer?** (A fair event entry form with God's name) **About what part of the Lord's Prayer does this remind us?** (The First Petition, "Hallowed be Thy name.")

Pray **Dear God, help us to keep Your name holy and glorify You as we live according to Your Word and shine like lights so others know You. And now we pray together the prayer Jesus taught us.** Conclude by praying the Lord's Prayer out loud together.

Direct the students to place their Lesson 6 fair ticket into their prayer wheel pocket. As each person leaves, say, **God helps us keep His name holy.**

Living the Faith

Encourage students to think of times when they can point out God's goodness. For example, when someone compliments a skill or talent they have, the students can praise God so others know the blessing is from Him.

Snack

Glory Cakes

Cake decorating is one of many fair competitions. Cakes are decorated in many colors and designs. Before class, bake cupcakes; leave unfrosted. Provide canned vanilla frosting and various colors of frosting gels and sprinkles for students to use to decorate their snacks, reminding them of the goodness and beauty of God. Use plastic knives for spreading frosting and other toppings. Let children decorate two, so they have one to share. We share God's glory!

Hallowed Be Thy Name

Directions: In each situation taking place on the fairgrounds below, the people involved are showing their faith in God and are keeping His name holy. Write the letter of the Bible passage from the box that best describes the action shown in the blank beneath each situation.

A. And now we thank You, our God, and praise Your glorious name. (1 Chronicles 29:13)
B. Oh give thanks to the Lord, for He is good; for His steadfast love endures forever! (Psalm 118:1)
C. Call upon Me in the day of trouble; I will deliver you, and you shall glorify Me. (Psalm 50:15)
D. To our God and Father be glory forever and ever. Amen. (Philippians 4:20)

Lesson 7

Paul and Silas in Prison

Acts 16:16–34—God works through me to make His kingdom grow.

Key Point

Through the witness of Paul and Silas to the Philippian jailer and his family, the kingdom of God grew. We ask that God help us live according to His Word and use us to extend His kingdom of grace.

Law/**Gospel**

Satan and my sinful flesh do not want to hallow God's name or let His kingdom come. **Through water and the Word, God gives me His Holy Spirit so that I believe His Word, live as a member of His kingdom of grace, and use my gifts to share His love in Jesus, extending His kingdom.**

Context

Paul's first missionary journey is recorded in Acts 13–14. He traveled with Barnabas into Asia Minor, but then felt compelled to return to Jerusalem for a council (AD 49) to discuss the relationship of Old Testament laws to the new Christian Church (Acts 15:1–35). After this council, he and Silas started from Antioch on the second missionary journey, going as far as Greece (Acts 15:36–18:22). On this journey, they revisited places from Paul's first trip until the Holy Spirit directed them on to Macedonia (16:6–10). There, Paul and Silas had an extensive stay in Philippi. While some received and believed their message, many were threatened by it. Some beat them and even threw them in jail.

Commentary

Paul and Silas were in the custom of visiting Jewish or Roman holy places and places of prayer in order to engage people with the Gospel of Jesus. They were going to such a place when a demon-possessed girl was crying out in public about their mission. She was proclaiming the truth about them that they were "servants of the Most High God" sent to proclaim the "way of salvation" (16:17). She did this day after day, and at first, Paul allowed it to happen. But after it became a nuisance, Paul cast out the spirit. This upset her owners because they earned money by her fortune-telling.

She was possessed not with the Holy Spirit, but rather with an evil spirit. Her owners were not faithful to Jesus, but rather made money from her predictions. Her owners accused Paul and Silas of offending Roman customs and laws. Paul and Silas were beaten with rods and thrown in jail. The jailer was ordered to keep them secure, so he placed them in the inner cells of the jail and bound them with chains.

Their faith was not dampened, and they relied on God's promises during this persecution; they were praying to God and singing hymns. The other prisoners were listening to them. About midnight, God released their chains and the chains of all the prisoners. He opened the doors to the cells, but no prisoner escaped. Perhaps the other prisoners were influenced by Paul's prayers and hymns along with the miraculous release of bonds.

When the jailer saw all the doors open, he assumed the prisoners had escaped. He knew that the penalty for this dereliction was death, so he decided to take his own life instead of waiting for the death sentence from his commander. But Paul stopped him. The jailer immediately knew who was responsible for the miraculous release and the fact that no one escaped. His reaction is one of repentance. He wants to be saved. He wants the faith that has such confidence in the face of trials and tribulations.

Paul and Silas had witnessed to the inmates and the jailer by their prayers and hymns in the face of trials and their patience in the midst of persecution.

After the jailer's confession of Christ, Paul and Silas baptized him and his entire family.

God causes His kingdom to grow in the most unusual earthly circumstances. By all outward indications, it was a bleak situation that looked hopeless for Paul and Silas. But the Lord turned it into an opportunity to expand His kingdom. He worked through Paul and Silas to bring the jailer and his household to faith.

The Holy Spirit is at work in prayers, in hymns, in Scripture, and in Baptism. He converts the heart to trust in God by grace and grants the ability to live godly lives here in this world and in heaven for eternity.

To hear an in-depth discussion of this Bible account, visit cph.org/podcast and listen to our Seeds of Faith podcast each week.

Lesson 7

Paul and Silas in Prison

Acts 16:16–34

Connections

Bible Words
The kingdom of God is at hand; repent and believe in the gospel. Mark 1:15

Faith Words
kingdom of God

Hymns and Songs
Before You, Lord, We Bow (*LSB* 966)

The Lord's Prayer (*AGPS* 173 or Director CD 10)

Our Father, Who from Heaven Above (*LSB* 766; Director CD 7)

Catechism
The Second Petition

We ask God to give us His Holy Spirit so that we believe His Word and lead godly lives as members of His kingdom of grace; bring many others into His kingdom of grace; [and] use us to extend His kingdom of grace. (Question 213)

Take-Home Point
God works through me to make His kingdom grow.

1 Opening (15 minutes)

Welcome

To Prepare: Provide vegetable seed packets—corn and at least three other types of garden produce. Try to include at least one type of vegetable with which students might not be familiar (e.g., okra, eggplant). You will also need a fresh ear of sweet corn still in its husk. Make copies of the Lesson 7 fair ticket (Director CD) and Resource Page 7, one per student. Also have copies of the fair tickets from Lessons 1–6 and "A Responsive Reading on Prayer" ready.

Sit behind the ticket window and greet students. Pass out Lesson 7 tickets.

Say **Welcome back to the Christian County Fair and to our Sunday School course, *Pray, Praise & Give Thanks: Jesus Teaches Us to Pray*.**

Invite the students to take out their Lesson 7 fair tickets.

Ask **At most fairs, people exhibit vegetables and flowers that they have grown. What kind of vegetable do you see on today's fair ticket?** (Corn)

Bring out the ear of sweet corn in its husk. Set it over a newspaper and begin to peel back the husk from the ear of corn. Show the students what's inside. Show the students the silk at the top of the ear of corn and on the ear itself.

Ask **What is this part of the corn called?** (Silk) **On an ear of corn, there is one piece of silk for every kernel. By the time it gets to us in the grocery store, a lot of the silk has fallen off or been removed. Guess how many kernels a typical ear of corn has.** (800!)

Open the corn seed packet and invite the students to handle the seeds.

MATERIALS NEEDED

1 Opening	2 God Speaks	3 We Live	4 Closing
Director CD Lessons 1–6 fair tickets (Director CD) (optional) Corn seed packet Newspaper (as floor/table covering) Ear of sweet corn still in husk Other vegetable seed packets Lesson 7 fair tickets (Director CD) Copies of "A Responsive Reading on Prayer" (Director CD or p. 12) Resource Page 7	Three index cards Bibles Map of Paul's missionary journeys (online or in a Bible) Student Leaflet 7	Activity Page 7 Bibles "Our Hope" card (Director CD) White cardstock Leather twine, tipped yarn, or plastic or nylon cord, 16-inch length per student Pony beads (yellow or gold, blue, red, white or white flower, black)	Director CD Lesson 7 fair tickets

Say **The corn plant from which the ear of corn came began as a tiny seed like this one. It takes several months from the time the seeds are planted until the ears of corn are ready to be harvested from tall corn stalks. Today in our lesson, we will learn about another kind of growing that God makes happen through us. But let's start with prayer and singing.** Move to the worship area of your classroom.

Web Activity: Locate and preview a time-lapse video of growing corn. As students view the video, have them watch for the development of the ears of corn on the stalks.

Teacher Tip

Take a moment to review what you've learned so far. Show fair tickets from Lessons 1–6. Have students look at the clues and recall what they remind us about regarding praying to God. For each ticket, the clue should remind them of the lesson's Take-Home Point as well as a main point from the lesson's Bible story.

Worship

Sing "Before You, Lord, We Bow" (*LSB* 966). This hymn emphasizes God's kingdom on earth and in heaven.

Invocation **In the name of the Father and of the Son and of the Holy Spirit. Amen.**

Hand out copies of "A Responsive Reading on Prayer" (Director CD or p. 12). Use the reading together.

A "Fair"ly Good Clue to Learn a Fact about Prayer

Say **The basket of corn on this lesson's ticket reminds us of things that grow. Besides plants, name other things that grow.** (People, animals, a bank account, debt, collections of items, a wildfire, knowledge, etc.) **When we pray the Lord's Prayer, we pray, "Thy kingdom come." In this Second Petition of the Lord's Prayer, we ask God to make His kingdom grow, and to work through us to make it grow. We'll find out more about this.**

Prayer at the Fair Opening Devotion

Hand out Resource Page 7.

Say **Let's find out what's going on with Emily as the fair begins its second day.** Ask volunteers to take turns reading out loud the devotion.

Ask **Whom did Emily invite to attend the fair with her and her parents?** (Her friend Zoey) **In what way did God work through Emily?** (He helped Emily show Zoey kindness by inviting her to the fair.) **In what way did God work through Emily's parents?** (God helped them show kindness to both Zoey and Emily by paying for their armbands.) **What did Emily's invitation to her friend do for the attendance numbers at the fair?** (The fair attendance grew even more due to Emily's invitation.)

Say **In our Bible story today, we will see how God worked through two friends named Paul and Silas. God used these friends in a very unusual place to offer a very special invitation to others. God used Paul and Silas to make His kingdom grow.**

Offering Encourage the students as they give their offerings. Offerings can be used by God to expand His kingdom.

Pray **Heavenly Father, as we study Your Word today, grow our faith in You. Help us to see how the Holy Spirit is at work in our lives to share God's grace with others. In Jesus' name we pray. Amen.**

Celebrate Recognize student birthdays, Baptism birthdays, and significant family events in your routine manner.

2 God Speaks (20 minutes)

God Teaches about Prayer

To Prepare: Have Bibles, Student Leaflet 7, and pencils ready for use. On three separate index cards, print the following Bible references, one reference per card: Acts 16:16–18; Acts 16:19–24; and Acts 16:25–34. Locate a map of Paul's missionary journeys, perhaps online or as a reference page in a Bible.

Direct the students to the Blue-Ribbon Bible Stories arena. Divide them into three groups. Hand out Bibles. Help everyone locate Acts 16:16. Bring out the map.

Say **Our Bible account today features two men, Paul and Silas. Directed by the Holy Spirit, they traveled to many places to spread the Gospel. Eventually, they came to Philippi.** Point it out on the map. **Paul and Silas hoped to talk to people about the saving love of Jesus. On their way, they had a peculiar encounter, which God used to work through them in an unusual way.** Give each group an index card and a pencil.

Say **Each of your groups has an index card that has a part of today's Bible story referenced on it. Read your part of the Bible story out loud together. On your index card, write down the main ideas and actions that take place in your section of the Bible story.**

Give each group five to seven minutes to read their portion of the Bible story and to note the main ideas. Then have them present their findings to the class, being sure to answer the following questions.

Ask **Our first group read the beginning of the Bible account, Acts 16:16–18. What happened first?** (The slave girl who kept crying out as she followed Paul and Silas had a spirit inside of her that could predict what would happen to people. Her owners used this ability to make money.) **What did the girl continue to cry out as she followed Paul and Silas?** (She said, "These men are servants of the Most High God, who proclaim to you the way of salvation" [v. 17]. Evil spirits can recognize God's work.)

Ask **At first, Paul allowed the spirit in the girl to continue to cry out. But finally, what did Paul do?** (By God's power, Paul called to the evil spirit to come out of the girl; at that very time, it left.) **What does this miracle healing tell you about God?** (God is mightier than anyone or anything. The name of Jesus is powerful.)

Ask **Our second group read the middle section, Acts 16:19–24. What happened after the evil spirit came out of the girl?** (Let group members share.) **When the girl's owners discovered she could no longer tell fortunes, what did they do to Paul and Silas?** (Accused them of causing a disturbance) **Why did the slave owners do this to Paul and Silas?** (The girl could no longer make money for her slave owners.)

Say **The crowd in the marketplace joined the rulers and judges in attacking Paul and Silas. The judges ordered that Paul and Silas be beaten.**

Ask **What happened next to the two men?** (Paul and Silas were thrown into jail. The jailer placed them in the inner area of the prison. He locked their feet in stocks so they could not walk or escape.)

Say **Our third group read Acts 16:25–34. Tell about what happened while Paul and Silas were imprisoned.** (Let group members share.)

Ask **What were Paul and Silas doing in the prison during the night?** (They prayed to God and sang hymns to Him.) **What were the other prisoners doing as Paul and Silas prayed and sang?** (They were listening to them.) **Even though they were in prison, God worked through Paul and Silas to tell others about Jesus through their prayers and songs. God can work through us to do His will no matter what circumstances we might be in!**

Ask **As Paul and Silas witnessed of Jesus to the other prisoners, what suddenly happened?** (There was a great earthquake. All the doors of the jail flew open, and all the chains and stocks the prisoners were in came open too.) **Why was the jailer in such a panic when this happened?** (According to Roman law, if a Roman guard lost his prisoners, he was to be killed.)

Ask **How did Paul reassure the jailer and prevent him from killing himself?** (Paul let the jailer know that none of the prisoners had escaped.) **What did he ask Paul and Silas?** ("Sirs, what must I do to be saved?" [v. 30]. In this question, the jailer confessed that he needed rescue from sin.) **What did Paul and Silas tell the jailer?** ("Believe in the Lord Jesus, and you will be saved, you and your household" [v. 31]. They spoke God's Word to the jailer and his entire family to tell them of Jesus' grace.)

Ask **How did the jailer react?** (He washed Paul and Silas's wounds. Then the jailer had Paul and Silas baptize him and his entire family. He invited Paul and Silas to eat dinner with him and his family [v. 34]. They were filled with joy because of the faith in God they received through Holy Baptism.)

Review

Hand out Student Leaflet 7 and pencils. Let students work with a partner to number the sentences in the correct order. **Answers:** 1, 4, 5, 7, 8, 9, 6, 3, 2.

Bible Words

The kingdom of God is at hand; repent and believe in the gospel. Mark 1:15

Locate the Bible Words on the student leaflet. Read them out loud together.

Write the Faith Words, *kingdom of God*, on the board.

Ask **When we pray the Lord's Prayer, we pray the words, "Thy kingdom come." What is the kingdom of God?** (God's reign as king over the whole universe, over the Church on earth, over the Church and angels in heaven)

Ask **For what do we ask God when we pray "Thy kingdom come"?** (We ask God to strengthen our faith in Him. We also pray that God would use us to tell others that Jesus is our Savior. We pray that God would enlarge His kingdom of grace—that more people would become a part of it. We pray that Jesus would hasten the coming of His kingdom of glory, because we eagerly await His second coming when all believers will be in heaven with Him.)

Teach these Bible Words using a two-clap rhythm as indicated by the *X*s in the verse below. The syllables in bold indicate where the accents should be.

The **king**dom of **God** is at **hand** (XX); re**pent** and be**lieve** in the **gos**pel (XX).

3 We Live (20 minutes)

Pray, Praise & Give Thanks

To Prepare: Make copies of Activity Page 7. Have pencils ready for use.

Have students get their Lord's Prayer page from their prayer wheel pocket.

Ask **The Second Petition of the Lord's Prayer is "Thy kingdom come." In today's Bible account, how did God use Paul and Silas to extend His kingdom of grace?** (God put Paul and Silas in the places they needed to be to share the Gospel and gave them the strength to do it.)

Ask **Do you think that Paul and Silas could have shared the Gospel on their own, without God's help and His strength?** (No. They had been beaten and were chained in the most secure part of the jail. And they would have had no desire to share the Gospel. But in Holy Baptism, they received the gift of the Holy Spirit, who helped them to share the Gospel.)

Say **Wherever Paul traveled, Satan tried to stop the spread of God's kingdom. Satan tries to stop us from sharing God's Word too. Satan can make us doubt that God really cares about us. He can try to trick us into believing that God's Word is not true. He can make us ignore the opportunities God gives us to share the Gospel. But by the power of the Holy Spirit, God gives us faith and keeps it strong. He helps us to live as members of God's kingdom and uses us to grow the kingdom.**

Hand out Activity Page 7. Have a volunteer read out loud the directions at the top of the page. Discuss each situation and how the Holy Spirit is working through the people to make His kingdom grow; then encourage the students to talk about the scene they drew and how God can work through *them.*

- God is using the girl to comfort the little boy by praying with him. In doing so, she is showing the boy that God cares for him.
- God is using these singers to share the truth of the grace and forgiveness He gives through faith in Jesus to a large crowd.
- God is using the woman to share His Word with someone else. Reading a Bible verse can provide an opportunity to share the Gospel.
- God is using this man to show another family God's kindness by paying their way to the fair. The man can use this opportunity to talk about grace and how salvation is a free gift of God through faith in Christ Jesus.
- Through the giving of the cross, God can use the pastor and boys to start a conversation about Jesus with others. God can help them boldly tell others that through faith in Jesus, we have forgiveness and eternal life.

At the end of this section of the lesson, have the students return their copies of the Lord's Prayer to their prayer wheel pocket.

Craft—Witness Bracelets

To Prepare: Provide a 16-inch length of leather twine or nylon cord for each child. Set out bowls of black, red, white, light blue, and yellow pony beads. If possible, use flower-shaped white (or clear) pony beads. Photocopy the "Our

Hope" card (Director CD) onto cardstock for each child.

Say **At a fair, you'll often find vendors who have made crafts to sell, and sometimes jewelry is part of an art contest at the fair. Let's try our own hand at jewelry making by creating a witness bracelet. Then "try your hand" at sharing the Gospel by giving the bracelet to someone else.**

Have the children string the beads onto the twine in the order below. When complete, have them center the line of beads and tie a knot on each end, holding them all in place. Finally, string both ends through the same two blue beads (in opposite directions). After the ends are through the beads, knot them so they won't go back through the beads.

Say **Each color reminds us of what we believe.** Show the "Our Hope" cards.

- **The first bead is black, because there is a black cross in the middle. We have faith in Jesus, who was crucified to pay the penalty for our sins.**
- **Add a red bead to show that the Holy Spirit makes us alive in Christ and gives us a clean heart through faith.**
- **Next, add two white beads** (or one white flower bead)**. The faith in our hearts given to us by the Holy Spirit gives us joy, comfort, and peace.**
- **Then add a blue bead to remind us that because of our faith, we have the hope of heavenly joy in the future.**
- **Finally, add a yellow bead to remind us that heaven's blessedness is precious, like gold. Heaven's joys are more valuable than any other treasure, and our joy will last forever.**

Teacher Tip

Encourage the children to use the bracelet as a way to tell friends about *Pray, Praise & Give Thanks*, and then invite them to come, so they can hear that Jesus loves them and is their Savior.

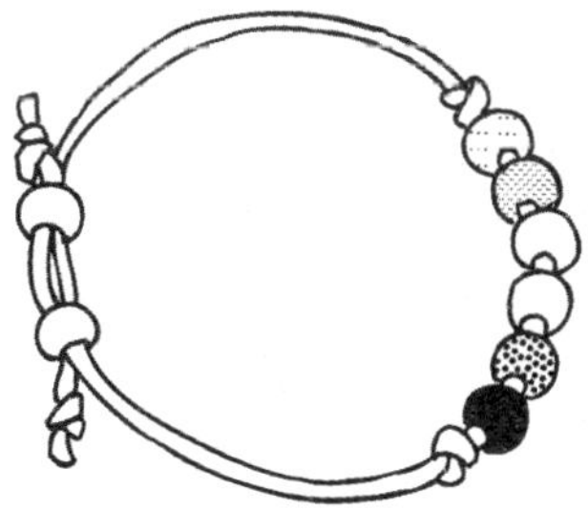

4 Closing (5 minutes)

To Prepare: Have your Lesson 7 fair ticket ready for use.

Sing "Lord's Prayer" (*AGPS* 173:1–3) or "The Lord's Prayer" (Director CD 10), or close with "Our Father, Who from Heaven Above" (*LSB* 766:3; Director CD 7).

Bring out the Lesson 7 fair tickets.

Ask **What is today's "fair"ly good clue about prayer?** (A basket filled with ears of corn)

Ask **This clue reminds us of things that grow. What did we talk about in today's lesson that the Holy Spirit makes grow?** (God's kingdom of grace)

Pray **Lord God, through water and the Word You have brought us into Your kingdom and given us eternal life in Your heavenly kingdom. Through the Holy Spirit, help us to share the Gospel with others. We pray together the prayer Jesus has taught us.** Conclude by praying the Lord's Prayer out loud together.

Direct the students to place their Lesson 7 fair ticket into their prayer wheel pocket. Make sure they have with them the Witness Bracelet they made to give to someone this week. As each person leaves, say, **God works through us to make His kingdom grow.**

Snack

Corny Treats

Serve a snack today which has corn as one of its major ingredients. Some suggestions are corn muffins or cornbread and jelly, kettle popcorn, corn nuts (crunchy toasted corn bits), or even small ears of corn on the cob with butter (reminiscent of the roasted corn cobs so popular at fairs), cooked for 4–6 minutes in the microwave with husks still on.

Living the Faith

Encourage the students to pray this week for the person to whom they give their bracelet so that he or she would know the Good News of Jesus.

Thy Kingdom Come

Directions: In the Lord's Prayer, we pray that God would use us and our sharing of the Gospel as He brings others to saving faith in Him. Carefully observe each situation pictured below. How is God using the people in these situations to make His kingdom of grace grow?

1.

2.

3.

4.

5.

6.

How might God use you to grow His kingdom? Draw a picture of it here.

Lesson 8

Preparing the Lesson

Job

Job 1:1–2:6; 42—God keeps me strong in faith.

Key Point

Despite all the troubles the devil threw at Job, God is faithful and did not allow the devil to destroy Job's faith. Amid the troubles we experience in our lives, God strengthens us through His Word and keeps us in faith to life everlasting.

Law/**Gospel**

The wages of sin is death. Troubles and suffering in this world come as a result of the fall into sin; affect all people, even God's children; and can make me falter, especially in adversity. **Jesus bore all of the punishment for sin on the cross, so there is none left for me to pay. God gives me strength through His Word to endure the troubles and sufferings that come to me in this life. He uses them to point me to Christ, working all things for my good and keeping me in faith to life everlasting.**

Context

Job is not a descendant of Abraham. He is not a child of God by nationality, but rather by faith. Scholars believe Job lived around 2000 BC in the land to the east of the Jordan. He was not connected to the patriarchs of Israel, and no mention is made of them in his book, but it is possible he lived at the same time as Abraham. Job is an example of hope for people not ethnically born in the Jewish line. God wants all people to have faith in Him and His mercy.

Commentary

The author of the book of Job states in the first few verses that Job was "blameless and upright, one who feared God and turned away from evil." God confirms this in speaking with Satan (1:8). The Holy Spirit caused this book to be written so that we could hear from God why bad things happen to good people. When God allows Satan to take Job's property and children, it seems as if God is evil, or at least gives in to Satan's evil plot.

If God is good and almighty, then why does sin exist and why do bad things happen? This is the problem of evil. It's a problem because it seems to contradict what the Bible says about God. What we know of God from Holy Scripture is that God is all-powerful, eternal, omniscient, just, and good. What we know about sin is that it entered the world through Adam and did not come from God (Romans 5:12).

It stands to our earthly reason that those who do bad receive punishment. When a car thief gets caught, just punishment means he should go to jail. But what baffles the human mind is that those who appear to be good have bad things happen to them. When the car thief steals the Smiths' only car while they're volunteering at a local food pantry, it doesn't seem like God is fair.

When Satan takes all of Job's possessions, his children, and his health, and Job's wife removes her support, Job is confronted with the problem of evil. He must wrestle with why God would allow this to happen to him. His three friends visit him and give their best answer to this problem: bad things do not happen to good people; you must not be good. Job flirts with another answer: God may not be good. Both of these answers contradict the Bible.

We know that all people are sinful, that no one earns God's favor, that no one is free from all guilt. But we are told in chapter 1 that Job did not earn this calamity. So Job's friends are wrong, even though he can't convince them. We know that God is righteous and good and is the judge of all from Psalm 7; Isaiah 45:21; and many other passages. So Job is wrong to think that he would win a court case with God if he went to trial (9:32–33). What we understand as good must be nuanced with the will of God. God's will is not for the death of the sinner (Ezekiel 33:11). He wants all to turn from their sin and live (1 Timothy 2:4). All trials and crosses in this world work for the good of those who love Him (Romans 8:28). God's will is to break and hinder every evil purpose of the devil, the world, and our sinful nature, which try to destroy our faith in Jesus, and to strengthen and keep us firm in His Word and faith until we die.

When we go through trials and crosses in this world, God is shaping and strengthening us. It is for our good so that we can see that He alone is our rock and our salvation. No one escapes this world alive. God prepares us to endure all manner of evil that might get in the way of faith.

In the end, God praises Job's faith and confession. Job spoke rightly about God (42:8). He confessed God as His Savior and addressed Him as His God throughout his trials.

To hear an in-depth discussion of this Bible account, visit cph.org/podcast and listen to our Seeds of Faith podcast each week.

Lesson 8

Job

Job 1:1–2:10; 42

Connections

Bible Words
For I know that my Redeemer lives. Job 19:25

Faith Words
God's will

Hymns and Songs
Come, My Soul, with Every Care (*LSB* 779; Director CD 2)

Our Father, Who from Heaven Above (*LSB* 766; Director CD 7)

The Lord's Prayer (*AGPS* 173 or Director CD 10)

We Praise You, O God (*LSB* 785; Director CD 11)

Catechism
The Third Petition

God's will is done when He breaks . . . the plans of the devil, the world, and our sinful nature, which try to destroy our faith . . . [and when He] keeps us firm in His Word and faith and helps us lead God-pleasing lives. (Question 218)

Take-Home Point
God keeps me strong in faith.

1 Opening (15 minutes)

Welcome

To Prepare: Before class, gather a small handheld weight. Make copies of the Lesson 8 fair ticket (Director CD) and Resource Page 8, one per student. Have copies of "A Responsive Reading on Prayer" ready for use.

Sit behind the ticket window and greet students. Pass out Lesson 8 tickets.

Say **Welcome back to the Christian County Fair. Today, we will continue to look at the petitions found in the Lord's Prayer.**

Bring out the handheld weight and do a few curls with your arm.

Ask **What is this item?** (Exercise weight) **Why do people use weights like these?** (To strengthen their body) Direct the students to look at their Lesson 8 fair ticket. **What is the prayer clue?** (A barbell) **What's next to the barbell on your ticket?** (A Bible with a cross on it) **Today, we will learn that God keeps us strong in faith. Let's continue with song and prayer.** Move to the worship area of your classroom.

Web Activity: Locate or have a student locate information about "fair strength test game." It is also known as the "high striker" or "strongman game." Discuss what is necessary to hit the bell at the top (physical strength and good aim).

Worship

Sing "Come, My Soul, with Every Care" (*LSB* 779; Director CD 2) or "Our Father, Who from Heaven Above" (*LSB* 766:4; Director CD 7). These songs

MATERIALS NEEDED

1 Opening	2 God Speaks	3 We Live	4 Closing
Director CD Small handheld weight Lesson 8 fair tickets (Director CD) Copies of "A Responsive Reading on Prayer" (Director CD or p. 12) Resource Page 8	Bibles Student Leaflet 8	Activity Page 8 Bibles Wooden dowel sticks, 1 per student Aluminum foil Black electric tape Small inflated balloons (black), 2 per student White paper Black and white paint (optional)	Director CD Lesson 8 fair tickets

emphasize trusting in God's will and in His strength.

Invocation **In the name of the Father and of the Son and of the Holy Spirit. Amen.**

Hand out copies of "A Responsive Reading on Prayer" (Director CD or p. 12).

A "Fair"ly Good Clue to Learn a Fact about Prayer

Invite the students to take out their Lesson 8 fair ticket again.

Ask **Earlier we noticed a Bible with a cross near the barbell. Why do you think it was placed there?** (Our strength comes from the Lord.)

Say **When we pray the Lord's Prayer, we pray, "Thy will be done on earth as it is in heaven." Praying for God's strength to do His will is an important part of this Third Petition of the Lord's Prayer. We'll find out why.**

Prayer at the Fair Opening Devotion

Hand out Resource Page 8.

Say **Let's find out how Emily and Zoey's armband day continued.** Ask volunteers to take turns reading out loud the devotion.

Ask **Why did Emily and Zoey need strength at the fair?** (A big storm blew in and frightened the girls.) **To whom did the girls turn for strength?** (They prayed to God to help them get to a place of shelter.)

Ask **How did God help the girls?** (God gave the girls faith to trust in Him and pray to Him even though they were scared. God worked through Emily's parents to alert the girls to the danger and to lead them to safety.)

Say **In today's Bible story, we will learn about a man who experienced some very terrible troubles in his life. We will see how God's will was done in this man's life and how God strengthened his faith.**

Offering Encourage the students as they give their offerings. Remind them that the money is used for things that strengthen people's faith.

Pray **Heavenly Father, as we study Your Word today, help us to see that You never fail to be with us and that You give us strength to face the difficult times in our lives. In Jesus' name we pray. Amen.**

Celebrate Recognize student birthdays, Baptism birthdays, and significant family events in your routine manner.

2 God Speaks (20 minutes)

God Teaches about Prayer

To Prepare: Have Bibles, Student Leaflet 8, and pencils ready for use.

Direct the students to the Bible story area and hand out Bibles.

Help the students locate Job 1:1. Ask a child to read verses 1–5.

Ask **Today's Bible account introduces us to a man named Job. What do these verses tell you about him?** (Job trusted in God. God had blessed Job with ten children and many animals and servants. Job was very rich. Job had a wonderful life, yet realized that he and his family were sinful. Through the sacrifices to God that Job offered, he sought God's forgiveness.)

Teacher Tip

Write *Job* on the board. Say, **Even though his name is spelled *J-O-B* and looks like the word that means "occupation," his name is pronounced with a long *O* sound.**

Ask another volunteer to read out loud Job 1:6–12.

Ask **One day Satan paid a visit to God. God spoke to Satan about Job and his faithfulness. What question does Satan ask God?** (Satan asked, "Does Job fear God for no reason?" Satan challenged the strength of Job's faith. He wondered if Job was trusting in God only *in order to* receive blessings. He wondered if Job would continue to trust even if the blessings were taken away.)

Ask **Look back at Job 1:12. What does God allow Satan to do to test Job?** (Take away all that Job has) **What does God *not* allow Satan to do to Job?** (Hurt Job physically)

Ask another volunteer to read out loud Job 1:13–22.

Ask **What did Satan do to Job?** (Destroyed all of Job's livestock, servants, and children) **What was Job's reaction to these disasters?** (Job mourned over his great loss, and yet he still blessed the name of the Lord. He realized that God both gives and takes away our belongings according to His holy and perfect will. Job did not accuse God of doing wrong, or curse God, as Satan thought he would.)

Say **So Satan returned to God. God told Satan how faithful Job remained despite all he had lost. So Satan devised another challenge to try to get Job to turn from God. Let's read Job 2:4–6.** Read the verses together.

Ask **What did Satan want to do to Job next?** (Hurt Job physically) **How did God limit Satan's plan?** (God told Satan he must not kill him.)

Ask a volunteer to read out loud Job 2:7–8.

Ask **How did Satan hurt Job?** (Satan struck Job with terrible sores that caused Job miserable suffering.) **Job's wife then told him that he should curse God for all the troubles he was experiencing. But Job did not. Why not?** (Job was faithful to God and trusted in Him.)

Ask **What could Job have done? Here's a hint: It's the same thing we can do whenever we have troubles.** (Job could have prayed to God and asked for His strength and help. God wants us to remember to call upon His name in every trouble and to remember that He has the power to help us.)

Say **As Job's story continued, he wrestled in his heart and mind with the problem of evil. He wondered why God would allow these bad things to happen to him. Job's friends gave Job bad advice about him and his relationship to God. Then Job questioned God and himself. God responded to Job's questions by reminding him of His power and His love. God mercifully led Job to the correct conclusion about Job's situation and His will. Let's read about it in Job 42.**

Help the students locate Job 42:1. Ask a volunteer to read verses 1–6.

Ask **In these verses, what did Job confess about God?** (That God can do all things. Job was sorry that he did not trust in God and His goodness.)

Ask a volunteer to read out loud verses 7–9.

Ask **Despite his friends' bad advice, what did Job do for them?** (Job prayed to God for them and asked God to forgive them. God did.)

Read out loud in unison verses 10–17.

Ask **How did God show His grace to Job?** (He gave Job twice as many possessions as before. He blessed Job with ten children and a long life.)

Review

Hand out Student Leaflet 8 and pencils. Work together as class to determine the truth of the statements on the page and to correct those which are not true. As a class, discuss which word in the sentence needs to be changed in order to make it a true statement. **Answers:** 1. False: Job **did** faithfully follow God; 2. True; 3. True; 4. True; 5. True; 6. False: Job **did** repent to God for questioning His will for him; 7. True; 8. False: God blessed Job with **ten** more children and **many** riches; 9. True.

Bible Words

For I know that my Redeemer lives. Job 19:25

Locate the Bible Words on the student leaflet. Read them out loud together.

Ask **Who is Job's Redeemer and ours?** (Jesus) **When in the Church Year do we often sing these words?** (Easter) **Why?** (We celebrate Jesus' resurrection.) **Why did Job say these words?** (God led Job to see that He only wanted good for him. God gave Job faith to believe that He would someday send a Savior who would die to pay the price we owed God for our sins and rise again to conquer sin, death, and Satan.) To teach these words, have the students sing the first stanza of the hymn "I Know That My Redeemer Lives" (*LSB* 461). If time permits, sing the rest of the hymn for an even richer understanding of what the phrase means.

3 We Live (20 minutes)

Pray, Praise & Give Thanks

To Prepare: Make copies of Activity Page 8. Provide pencils and Bibles.

Have students gather their copy of the Lord's Prayer (Activity Page 4) from their prayer wheel pocket. Direct the students to the Third Petition and read it aloud together. Write the Faith Words, *God's will*, on the board.

Say **God's will is that His name be kept holy and that His kingdom come, as we prayed about in the First and Second Petitions. God's will is that people would teach His Word correctly and that all people will know that Jesus is their Savior, and then that they would remain in that faith through the Holy Spirit and lead God-pleasing lives according to it.**

Ask **In Job's life, who tried to stop God's will for him?** (Satan, the world, and his own sinful nature) **In our lives, who tries to stop God's will?** (Satan, the world, and our own sinful natures)

Ask **How did God stop evil from destroying Job's faith in Him?** (God did not let Satan end Job's life, and when Job had questions and doubts, God reminded Job of His power over all things. God reminded Job of the truth of His Word and gave him strength so that his faith in God was not destroyed.)

Say **God also does this for *us*. In God's Word, we see how God has power over all things. He strengthens us through His Word and Sacraments so that temptations from Satan, the world, and our own sinful flesh do not destroy our faith.**

Through faith in Jesus, we have eternal life. We read and hear the truth that Jesus died on the cross and rose again to rescue us from sin and eternal death. By the power of the Holy Spirit, God gives us strength to live according to His will for us, no matter what happens to us in this life.

Say **Adam and Eve's first sin brought death into God's perfect creation. God is just. Therefore, He kept His Word when He told Adam and Eve that the result of their sin would be death. But God is also love. When He created the world, it did not include death. But even before Adam and Eve sinned, God had a plan to save the human race from eternal death. According to God's Word, God "desires all people to be saved and to come to the knowledge of the truth"** (1 Timothy 2:4). **This is why we come together in Sunday School and church to learn more about Him and to receive His gifts of forgiveness and salvation** (eternal life).

Say **Sometimes people mistakenly feel that God is being mean to them by allowing bad things to happen in their lives. As God's children, He reassures us in 1 Corinthians 10:13, "No temptation has overtaken you that is not common to man. God is faithful, and He will not let you be tempted beyond your ability, but with the temptation He will also provide the way of escape, that you may be able to endure it."**

Ask **Let's review. Do you remember how God changed the bad situation?** (In Genesis 3:15, God promised to send a Savior. Through His death and resurrection, Jesus carried out God's will to stop every evil purpose of the devil, the world, and our sinful nature. Through faith in Jesus, we are saved!)

Ask **So why did God allow troubles to come to Job? And why does He allow troubles to come to us?** Discuss.

Say **God worked through the difficulties Job experienced to strengthen his faith. God allows us to go through troubles for the same reason: to strengthen our faith. God uses difficulties to lead us to rely on Him and trust in His goodness and His strength, not our own. God tells us in His Word, "For those who love God all things work together for good, for those who are called according to His purpose"** (Romans 8:28). **God promises to always be with us and to answer our prayers for help.**

Hand out Activity Page 8. Ask a volunteer to read out loud the directions. Beginning with Ephesians 6:10–13 at the bottom of the strength tester, locate and read each Bible passage together. On the line opposite each Bible reference, summarize what the passage says about God's strength.

- **Ephesians 6:10–13:** God's might and strength are what make us strong. God gives us armor (protection) to stand up against the devil and his schemes (e.g., faith in Jesus our Savior, the truth of His Word, and the power of the Holy Spirit, who helps us to pray to God at all times).
- **Psalm 105:4–5:** God leads us to look to Him and His strength. All He has done reminds us of His power and of His love for us.
- **Psalm 46:1:** God is our safe place and strength. He is there to help us.
- **Romans 8:38–39:** No trouble or problem can separate us from God's love for us in Christ Jesus.
- **Philippians 4:13:** With God's strength, we can do all things.

Ask **Which of these passages is especially meaningful to you as you face trouble in this world?** (Encourage students to share their choice.) **Why is**

prayer so important when we face troubles? (When we pray to God, we communicate with Him our fears and our needs. When we pray, we turn to God and ask Him to do what is best for us, according to His will.)

Have students place their Lord's Prayer page in their prayer wheel pocket.

Craft—God Gives Strength Barbells

To Prepare: Provide a wooden dowel rod, paper, and two small, inflated black balloons for each child. Have foil, scissors, and black electrical tape (or clear packing tape) ready for use. Black and white paint with brushes is optional. You may choose to prepaint the dowel rods black before class, instead of having the children wrap it in foil. *Note:* If any of your students are allergic to latex, use small, round black mylar (foil) balloons that are already filled with compressed air. Another option is to spray paint small play balls black.

Say **Let's make a barbell to remind us that God keeps us strong in faith, even when troubles come our way.**

Give each person a dowel, scissors, foil, and electric tape. Direct each student to cover their dowel rod with the foil and tape it securely. Give each student two inflated balloons. Have them tape the tied (fastened) end of a balloon at to the dowel, one at each end. Adjust the balloons to look like weights. Tape a white cross made out of paper to the balloon weights (or paint one).

Say **Gently tape** (or paint) **a cross on each balloon to remind you that our faith and source of strength is in Jesus, our Savior and Redeemer.**

4 Closing (5 minutes)

To Prepare: Have your Lesson 8 ticket.

Sing "Lord's Prayer" (*AGPS* 173:1–4) or "The Lord's Prayer" (Director CD 10), or close with "We Praise You, O God" (*LSB* 785; Director CD 11).

Bring out the Lesson 8 fair tickets.

Ask **What does a barbell remind you about God's strength?** (Through His Word and Sacraments, God gives us faith in Jesus and keeps us strong in that faith no matter what troubles we may face. That's God's will!)

Pray **Almighty God, through the strength of Your Son, Jesus, You have rescued us from sin, death, and Satan. Thank You for the faith You have given us in Jesus, our Redeemer, and keep us forever in that faith despite the troubles we may face. We pray together the prayer that Jesus taught us.** Conclude with the Lord's Prayer.

As each person leaves, say, **God keeps us strong in faith.**

Living the Faith

Encourage students to place their "God Gives Strength Barbells" somewhere at home where they will see them often. Encourage them to memorize one of the strength Bible verses from Activity Page 8 as a reminder that God is with them and keeps their faith strong at all times.

Snack

Power Mix

Strong men (and women) need healthy grains and fruits to stay in shape. In colorful paper cups, serve a mixture of dried fruits, chocolate chips, and granola to strengthen the children as they faithfully follow the Lord. Another option (if logistically manageable and safe) is to make funnel cakes or hot cakes. Talk about how we can be in difficult situations (like the dough or batter being cooked), but God turns it into something good (like the delicious cooked dough/batter).

Thy Will Be Done on Earth as It Is in Heaven

Directions: God's will is done in our lives when He keeps the devil, the world, and our sinful nature from destroying our faith in Jesus, and when He strengthens and keeps us strong in His Word and helps us lead God-pleasing lives.

God keeps us strong in faith. On the strength tester game below are listed Bible references that tell us of God's strength. Locate each passage in your Bible and read it carefully. On the line next to the reference, summarize what the passage says about the strength God gives us.

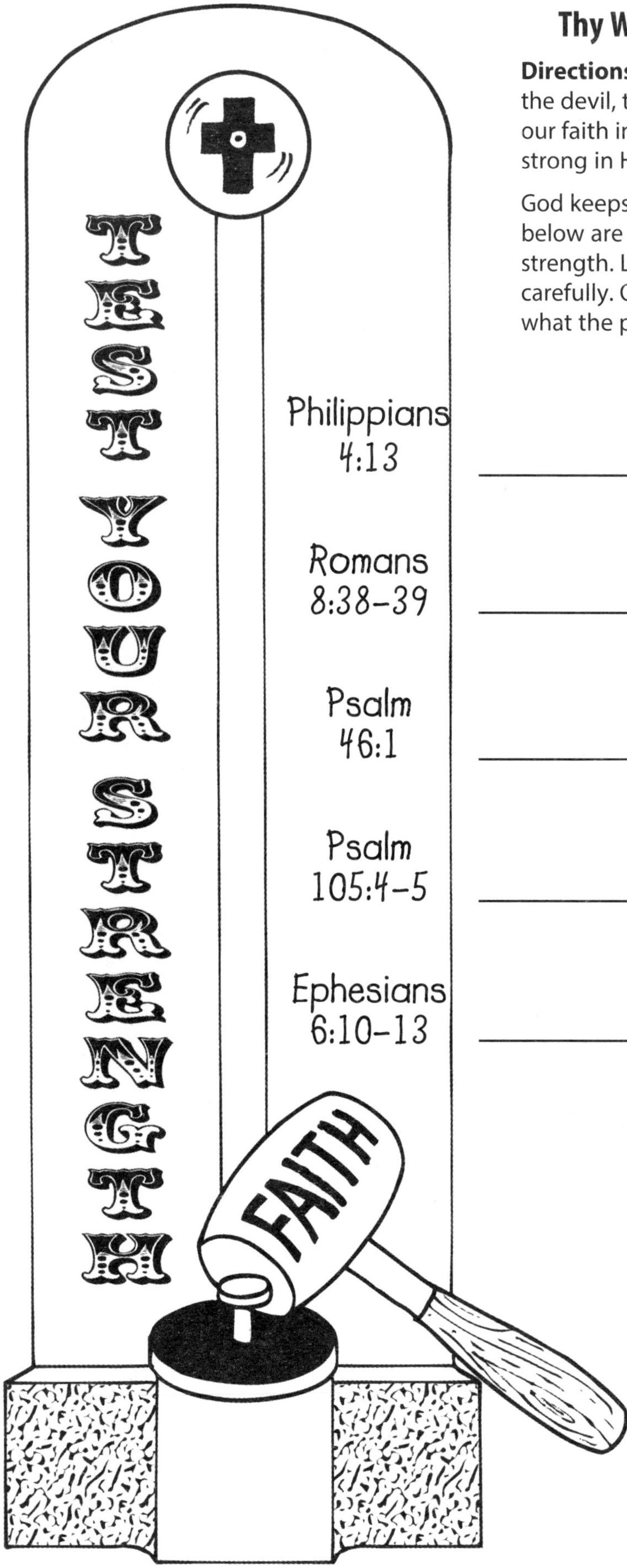

Lesson 9

Preparing the Lesson

God Provides Manna and Quail

Exodus 16—God gives me what I need.

Key Point

God provided for the children of Israel. We can trust God to provide all that we need.

Law/**Gospel**

According to my sinful nature, I quickly forget God's promises and power. When I think I lack food, money, a good job, or other First Article gifts included in "daily bread," I am tempted to think that God either does not love me, does not care, or can't provide what I need. **In Jesus, God came in the flesh to lead me out of slavery to sin to be with Him in the promised land of heaven. He promises He will never leave me or forsake me, but will supply all that I need**.

Context

Moses led the children of Israel out of their slavery in Egypt through the Red Sea. They were now in the Sinai Desert, where there was no food or water. God led them up against the Red Sea when the Egyptians were pursuing them so that He could show them His power. And by a mighty miracle, He delivered them out of the hand of Pharaoh and his army. From there, He led them into the desert so He could show them that He was the almighty God who could provide for their needs. He was with them in the pillar of cloud by day and the pillar of fire by night. He talked to them through His servant Moses.

Commentary

The children of Israel grumbled against the Lord in the desert. This means that they despised what He had done for them and wished He had left them alone in Egypt. They longed to be back in slavery, the very place where they cried out to the Lord for deliverance. They wanted to be rescued, but they did not trust God to give them good things. They were worried that God would not meet their needs.

Over and over again, the children of Israel are a picture of sinful man. They don't trust God, they grumble, they complain, they don't remember God's gracious actions toward them, they don't trust the leaders that God places over them, they doubt that God can provide for their needs, and they want a god after their own imagination. But God does not leave them or forsake them. He shows His power, His concern, His love, and His patience through His chosen leader. Moses is a picture of Christ. He is the mediator between God and Israel. When God grows angry and impatient, it is Moses who intercedes and reminds God of His promises. Sinful Israel needs Moses to intercede for them.

When they grumble for food, God provides a miracle. While wandering in the desert, the people could not grow food, so God provided it. He sent bread from heaven in the morning. When the people saw it for the first time, they asked, "What is it?" (Exodus 16:15). The word *manna* (16:31) means "what is it?" in Hebrew.

The people were to gather an omer, about two quarts, of manna in the morning. They were supposed to eat it that very day. They were not to leave any of it until the next morning. God gave a specific law regarding this that they did not obey. After the first day, it grew worms and stank. Again, they did not trust God to keep His Word. On the sixth day, they were to gather twice as much so that they could eat on the Sabbath. For on the Sabbath, God would not send any manna. Some of them did not obey this law either and went out to try and gather manna on the Sabbath.

God wanted to teach them to obey Him and to trust in Him. He was showing them that He would provide for their daily needs, literally their "daily bread." He also taught them to keep the Sabbath holy by resting on it and not working.

Jesus would use the analogy of manna, bread from heaven (16:4), to describe Himself in John 6:31-35. As bread sustains the body, so faith in Jesus sustains the soul. God provides both for the body and for the soul. He does not care for one at the expense of the other. In the Lord's Prayer, we pray for both body and soul. In the first three petitions, we pray for God to hallow His name, let His kingdom come, and let His will be done. These all integrate faith and action, Word and work. In the Fourth Petition, we pray that God would keep His promise to take care of our bodies and all things needed for this earthly life. Our Creator knows what we need even better than we do. He created us, He sent His Son to redeem us, He counts our hairs, and He has promised to sustain us in this world.

To hear an in-depth discussion of this Bible account, visit cph.org/podcast and listen to our Seeds of Faith podcast each week.

Lesson 9

God Provides Manna and Quail

Exodus 16

Connections

Bible Words
The eyes of all look to You, and You give them their food in due season. You open Your hand; You satisfy the desire of every living thing. Psalm 145:15–16

Faith Words
daily bread

Hymns and Songs
Now Thank We All Our God (*AGPS* 181; *LSB* 895)
What a Friend We Have in Jesus (*LSB* 770; Director CD 13)
Psalm 145:15–16 (Director CD 8)
The Lord's Prayer (*AGPS* 173 or Director CD 10)
Come, My Soul, with Every Care (*LSB* 779; Director CD 2)

Catechism
The Fourth Petition
We pray to God for daily bread . . . because Christ wants us to realize that our entire life . . . depends on God [and] look to God for physical as well as spiritual blessings. (Question 219)

Take-Home Point
God gives me what I need.

1 Opening (15 minutes)

Welcome

To Prepare: Before class, invite a member of your congregation who does home canning to come to your class with canning supplies and some of his or her finished products. You will need a jar of home-canned food, copies of the Lesson 9 fair ticket (Director CD), copies of "A Responsive Reading on Prayer" (Director CD or p. 12), and copies of Resource Page 9, one per student.

Sit behind the ticket window and greet students. Pass out Lesson 9 tickets.

Say **Welcome back to the Christian County Fair and to our Sunday School course, *Pray, Praise & Give Thanks: Jesus Teaches Us to Pray.* Today, we'll look at the Fourth Petition of the Lord's Prayer, "Give us this day our daily bread." First, let's learn how some of the food we eat is processed.**

Introduce your guest to the students, and gather around his or her supplies.

Ask **Have you ever eaten any home-canned food?** (Students share.) **For hundreds of years, gardeners have canned the vegetables and fruits they grow to provide food for their families. One process used to preserve the food is called water bath canning. It keeps food fresh and safe.**

Show the canning supplies. Invite the guest to briefly explain how foods are canned (e.g., cleaning the jars, keeping them warm, cooking the food that goes into them, filling them, getting rid of air bubbles, wiping the rims, adding the lid and band, using the water bath, sealing and storing them).

MATERIALS NEEDED

1 Opening	2 God Speaks	3 We Live	4 Closing
Director CD Jar of home-canned food (e.g. pickles, jelly, peaches) Empty canning jar, lid, and band Lesson 9 fair tickets (Director CD) Copies of "A Responsive Reading on Prayer" (Director CD or p. 12) Resource Page 9 Special guest to visit classroom (optional)	Bibles Student Leaflet 9 Director CD	Activity Page 9 Bibles Empty glass jars, 1 per student Paintbrushes Glow-in-the-dark paint Paper plates Table covering 1 × 5-inch strips of white index cards or cardstock Small plastic bags Paint smocks (optional)	Director CD Jar of home-canned food Lesson 9 fair ticket Daily Bread Strips (see Craft)

Say **We need to eat nutritious foods to live. Today, we'll see that God gives us what we need. Let's continue with worship.**

Web Activity: If you couldn't find someone to explain what they do, show a jar of home-canned food. Watch an appropriate online video demonstration of the water bath canning process.

Worship

Sing "Now Thank We All Our God" (*AGPS* 181; *LSB* 895) or "What a Friend We Have in Jesus" (*LSB* 770; Director CD 13) to emphasize the bountiful ways in which God gives us what we need.

Invocation **In the name of the Father and of the Son and of the Holy Spirit. Amen.**

Hand out copies of "A Responsive Reading on Prayer" (Director CD or p. 12). Use the reading together.

A "Fair"ly Good Clue to Learn a Fact about Prayer

Invite the students to take out their Lesson 9 fair ticket.

Ask **What "fair"ly good clue to learn about prayer do you see on your ticket?** (A jar of home-canned pickles) **Food is one important blessing that God gives us. God gives us other blessings too. The Fourth Petition of the Lord's Prayer calls all the blessings God gives us "daily bread."**

Write the Faith Words, *daily bread*, on the board.

Say **Throughout this lesson, we will find out more about the daily bread for which we ask God in prayer.**

Prayer at the Fair Opening Devotion

Hand out Resource Page 9.

Ask **If you were here for our last lesson, you'll remember that to escape the heavy rain, Emily, Zoey, and Emily's parents gathered inside the exhibition building at the fairgrounds. Let's find out about what they saw on display in the building as they waited for the storm to pass.**

Ask volunteers to take turns reading out loud the devotion.

Ask **What blessings from God did Emily, Zoey, and her parents see inside the exhibition building?** (Harvested vegetables from gardens throughout their county and home-canned pickles) **The food they saw at the fair reminded Emily, Zoey, and Emily's parents of other blessings God gives us. What else did they mention?** (Clothing, friendship, protection from the storm, and parents)

Say **In today's Bible story, we will find out how God blessed and provided for the children of Israel as they traveled to the land of Canaan. We will learn about the special "daily bread" God gave them.**

Offering Encourage the students as they give their offerings. Offerings give thanks to God for all of His blessings.

Pray **Dear heavenly Father, You are so good to us! As we study Your Word today, help us to give thanks to You for giving us what we need. In Jesus' name we pray. Amen.**

Celebrate Recognize student birthdays, Baptism birthdays, and significant family events in your routine manner.

2 God Speaks (20 minutes)

God Teaches about Prayer

To Prepare: Have Bibles, Student Leaflet 9, and pencils ready for use.

Direct the students to the Bible story arena. Hand out Bibles. Help the students to locate Exodus 16. Select three volunteers to play the special parts in the story. Have one person read God's words (16:4b–5, 12, 28b–29), one person read Moses' words (Exodus 16:6b–8, 9b, 15b–16, 19b, 23b, 25–26, 32–33), and one person read Aaron's words (Exodus 16:6b–7). The rest of the students will be the Israelites and can read the group parts (Exodus 16:3b, 15). You will serve as story narrator, reading the rest of the verses, and at the proper points in the Bible story, cue the actors to read their dialogue directly from the Bible.

Teacher Tip

Write the verse references on the board, so students can highlight their parts ahead of time.

Say **As this lesson's Bible story begins, a man named Moses and his brother Aaron are leading the children of Israel in the Sinai desert. God had recently done an amazing miracle when He parted the Red Sea so the Israelites could get away from Egypt, where they had been slaves.**

Ask **What do you know about the environment in a desert?** (It is very dry and hot. Little food, if any, grows there. Water is very limited.) **Bible scholars estimate that Moses likely led between two and three million people through the desert. What kinds of problems do you think Moses encountered along the way?** (Let students speculate. Moses and the people left Egypt with few food supplies. Some Bible scholars estimate that to feed the large number of Israelites just for one day would likely require at least a thousand tons of food and more than ten million gallons of water.)

Say **Let's find out what happened as God's people wandered in the desert wilderness.** Read verses 4–5.

Ask **Why were the Israelites complaining?** (They were hungry and had no food; they figured they would die.) **How did God answer the complaints of His people?** (God told Moses that every day He would provide "bread from heaven" for the people to eat. On the sixth day of each week, Friday, they were to gather twice as much bread.) Read Exodus 16:6–8.

Ask **Why were the complaints of the Israelites actually complaints against God Himself?** (It showed their lack of trust in God to provide for their needs. When the Israelites complained to Moses, God's representative, they were complaining against God's plans for them.) Read Exodus 16:9–12.

Ask **What did God tell Moses the people would eat?** (Bread in the morning and meat in the evening) **What did God want His people to know?** (He was giving them what they needed to live.) Read Exodus 16:13–21.

Ask **What kind of meat did God provide for His people each evening?** (Quail, a type of bird) **What happened when the people gathered more bread than what they needed?** (The extra bread would spoil.) **Why was Moses angry when the people did this?** (By gathering more bread than they could eat, the people disobeyed God's command. It showed they did not trust in God to provide for them what they needed each day.) Read Exodus 16:22–26.

Ask **Why did God command the people to gather twice as much bread on the sixth day, Friday, the day before the Sabbath Day?** (The Sabbath

Day was set aside from the time of creation as a day of rest. To gather or prepare food on the Sabbath Day was considered work.) Read Exodus 16:27–30.

Ask **What happened when some people went out to gather bread on the Sabbath Day?** (There wasn't any bread.) Read Exodus 16:31–36.

Say **The bread the people gathered each morning was called *manna*. *Manna* is what the words, "What is it?" sound like in the Hebrew language. The people likely ground the manna into flour to make bread.**

Ask **What did the manna taste like?** (Wafers made with honey) **An *omer* is an amount of about two quarts or liters. Why do you think God wanted the people to keep a sample of the manna?** (To remind them of God's daily care for them as they traveled in the wilderness) **For how long did the people eat manna?** (For forty years, until they came to the Promised Land)

Review

Direct each student to find a partner. Hand out Student Leaflet 9 and pencils. Have partners work together to solve the coded words in the Search & Know activity on page 4 of the student leaflet. **Answers:** 1. Moses, Egypt; 2. grumbled; 3. trust; 4. bread, meat; 5. manna, quail; 6. Sabbath; 7. remember.

Bible Words

The eyes of all look to You, and You give them their food in due season. You open Your hand; You satisfy the desire of every living thing. Psalm 145:15–16

Locate the Bible Words on the student leaflet. Help the students learn the words by singing "Psalm 145:15–16" (Director CD 8) or by doing this activity. Divide the Bible Words into four sections by circling each phrase. Ask the children to briefly describe the water cycle, then talk about the continuous "cycle" of God's care. Draw a simple diagram on the board as you read through each part of the verse. Draw a crowd of people (a bunch of circles) at the bottom of the board, with dots for eyes. / Draw an arrow coming down from heaven to the people. / Draw an open hand at the bottom of the arrow. / Draw smiley faces on the people. Add an arrow from the people up to heaven. We respond in trust and thankfulness!

3 We Live (20 minutes)

Pray, Praise & Give Thanks

To Prepare: Make copies of Activity Page 9. Have pencils ready.

Have students get their copy of the Lord's Prayer from their pocket.

Ask **How did the children of God react when they were faced with the challenges of traveling in the desert?** (They complained. They didn't trust God to take care of them, even though He just saved them from slavery.)

Ask **What are some times or situations when people your age complain?** (Wanting different food, wanting to be taken places, being bored, etc.) **When do people of all ages complain?** (When we are hungry, when we are scared, when we are sick, when we are worried, etc.)

Say **The root cause of all of our grumbling and complaining is our sinful**

nature. When we are faced with challenges in our lives, we often forget God's promises to care for us. We allow our fears and worries to fill our thoughts. We forget the many times God has powerfully proven by His actions in our lives that He will, indeed, provide all that we need.

Ask **What are some things that God has done for you in your life that prove that you can trust Him to give you what you need?** Write the responses on the board; you will use these later in the craft project.

Say **We have many, many needs. Physical needs are things associated with our body, such as clothing, food, shelter, safety, and health. We also have emotional needs. We need the love and supportive care of others so that we can be happy and live confidently. God provides people like police officers, firefighters, doctors, and our family members to help provide for our physical and emotional needs.**

Add new items from this list to the list the students previously compiled.

Ask **Is there anything missing from our list? What is our greatest need that only God can meet for us?** (To be rescued from our sins) **How did God meet this need for us?** (He sent Jesus, His Son, to die and rise again to save us from our sins and to give us eternal life through faith in Him.)

Ask **Why did God send Jesus to rescue us?** (God sent Jesus because He loves us. God knows that we cannot escape the slavery of sin on our own. So from the very first sin that Adam and Eve committed, God showed His grace and mercy for all people by promising to send a Savior to crush Satan.)

Say **In Jesus, God came in the flesh to lead us out of the slavery of sin so that we can be with Him in the promised land of heaven. Through faith in Jesus, God forgives all of our sins, including the times we don't trust in His care. Because God did this for us, we can be certain that He will never leave us, and He will always take care of all of our other needs.**

Have students bring out their copy of the Lord's Prayer. Help them find the Fourth Petition, "Give us this day our daily bread." Read it out loud together.

Say **God led the children of Israel out of slavery in Egypt. As they traveled in the desert, God fed them *every day*. According to Luther's Small Catechism, "daily bread includes everything that has to do with the support and needs of the body." In the catechism, there is a list of what daily bread is: "food, drink, clothing, shoes, house, home, land, animals, money, goods, a devout husband or wife, devout children, devout workers, devout and faithful rulers, good government, good weather, peace, health, self-control, good reputation, good friends, faithful neighbors, and the like."** Compare to your list and add any missing items.

Hand out Activity Page 9.

Say **In this fairground scene, there are fifteen different examples of the daily bread God gives us. See if you can find and circle them all.** **Answers:** 1. A food stand (food). 2. A livestock pen with goats (animals). 3. A police officer standing on patrol near the entrance (good workers, good government, peace). 4. The sun (good weather). 5. Two friends riding on the merry-go-round (friends). 6. A mom holding a young child's hand (parents). 7. A politician shaking hands of potential voters (good government). 8. A first-aid tent (health). 9. Two girls trying on baseball caps (clothes). 10.

A worker taking out a bag of trash (good workers). 11. An exhibit of home-canned foods (food). 12. A boy feeding a calf inside a livestock pen (animals). 13. A father purchasing tickets (money, parents). 14. A group of boys and girls waiting to ride the Ferris wheel (friends). 15. A young married couple holding hands (devout husband and wife).

Have students place the Lord's Prayer back into their prayer wheel pocket.

Craft—Daily Bread Jar

To Prepare: Cover the work area. If possible, provide smocks for the children. Provide for each child a paintbrush, plastic sandwich bag, and a clean glass jar (ideally quart size, but any size, including baby-food size, will do). Set out glow-in-the-dark paint and paper plates.

Ask **What did God ask the people to do so they would remember His care for them in the desert?** (Save some of the manna in a jar) **Let's make some "daily bread jars" to help remind us how God gives us what we need.**

Hand out the quart jars. Squirt a heap of paint onto a paper plate. Model how to dip the paint brush into the paint and use the tip to make small dots close together (but not touching) on the *inside* of the jar. Have students start at the bottom of the jar and work their way up, until the entire inside is covered. Set aside the jars to dry. (Sunlight will charge glow-in-the-dark paint.)

Give each student 7–10 index card strips and a pen. Have them write out examples of daily bread from the list you compiled earlier, one example per strip. Keep them in a bag, and when the jar has dried, place the bag inside.

Teacher Tip

Another option is to decoupage the jar using tissue paper pieces and a glue wash.

4 Closing (5 minutes)

To Prepare: Have a Lesson 9 ticket. Have the students bring their craft bags.

Sing "Lord's Prayer" (*AGPS* 173:1–4) or "The Lord's Prayer" (Director CD 10), or use "Come, My Soul, with Every Care" (*LSB* 779; Director CD 2).

Have the students look at the "fair"ly good clue about prayer on the ticket.

Ask **What does this jar of pickles tell you about what God gives you?** (God gives us our daily bread. Every day God gives us what we need.)

Pray **Heavenly Father, we thank You for Your grace and mercy, that you lead us out of our slavery of sin to be with You in the promised land of heaven. Each day along the way, You also give us our daily bread. Today, we thank You for . . .** (have each student take out a daily bread example from their bag and take turns saying them aloud)**. Thank You for giving us what we need. We pray together the prayer that Jesus taught us.** Conclude by praying the Lord's Prayer together.

Direct the students to place their Lesson 9 ticket into their prayer wheel pocket. As each person leaves, say, **God gives us what we need.**

Snack

Jars of Goodness

Provide a clean half-pint canning jar (or disposable bowl) for each child. Prepare a cereal buffet by pouring at least four different kinds of breakfast cereal into separate serving bowls. Have the students select several different cereals from the buffet and use a scoop to layer the cereals inside their jar. Provide milk and spoons. Talk about the different grains from which the cereals are made, and thank God for the farmers and good weather provided in order to grow the grain. Like the Israelites, we can be sure of God's care each morning too.

Living the Faith

Encourage the children to set their Daily Bread Jar in a place where they will see it every day, morning and evening. When they pray, they can take out one of the strips from the jar and thank God for that example of daily bread.

Give Us This Day Our Daily Bread

Directions: In the fairground scene below are fifteen different people and items that can be defined as "daily bread." Circle each example of daily bread that you find. See if you can find them all.

Lesson 10

Preparing the Lesson

Joseph Forgives His Brothers

Genesis 37:12–36; 45:1–15; 50:15–21—God forgives me and wants me to forgive others.

Key Point

Despite their sins against him, Joseph forgave his brothers. Despite our sins, God forgives us for Jesus' sake and wants us to forgive others.

Law/**Gospel**

The devil, the world, and my sinful nature war against me every day. I can't control what other people do to me or love and forgive them as I should. **Jesus, the sinless Son of God, suffered and died at the hands of evil men in order to earn salvation for the whole world. God forgives my sins for Jesus' sake and helps me to forgive others.**

Context

God had chosen Abraham and brought him out of Ur of the Chaldeans to be the father of His people. His son, Isaac, miraculously born in his parents' old age, was the first step. Isaac in turn had two sons, Jacob and Esau. Jacob went to his uncle Laban's country and married Leah and Rachel. Jacob had ten sons through Leah. Through Rachel, he had Joseph and later Benjamin. Jacob loved Rachel more than Leah and thus loved Joseph more than the ten sons of Leah. He treated Joseph with favor and gave him gifts and attention more than the others. Joseph boasted of dreams that his family would bow down to him. His brothers hated him.

Commentary

The story is a familiar one to most of us. Jacob sent Joseph to check on his brothers, who were tending the flocks in a nearby land. His brothers saw him coming and plotted to kill him. Instead, they sold Joseph to a caravan of traders on their way to Egypt. They covered up their sin by telling their father that they had found Joseph's blood-stained coat lying in a field. Jacob mourned inconsolably for Joseph, thinking that he was dead.

In Egypt, Joseph was sold to Potiphar, captain of Pharaoh's guard. Joseph was now alone, bound to a life of slavery, and away from his family because his brothers hated him and wanted him dead. God caused Joseph to rise through the ranks of his fellow servants. Even when falsely accused and thrown into jail, he was successful. By the hand of the Lord, Joseph was promoted to second-in-command for all of Egypt, in charge of distributing food to all people, both Egyptians and foreigners.

Because there was a drought in all the region, Joseph's brothers were forced to come buy grain in Egypt. Joseph was able to cause his brothers stress and remind them of what they had done to him. When they acknowledged their sin, he revealed himself to them and acted kindly toward them. He rescued them from the famine and brought his whole family to Egypt, giving them the best of the land to live in and to raise their flocks.

After all the evil that his brothers did to him, and after all the years that Joseph had to suffer because of their evil hatred, Joseph confesses that God sent him before them into Egypt to keep a remnant alive (45:7). He could see clearly that it was not his brothers who forced him to Egypt, but rather God who foresaw all the good that He would work through Joseph for the sake of the Messiah's lineage. The brothers meant it for evil, but God meant it for Joseph's good and, ultimately, the good of the whole world (50:20).

God's love filled Joseph's heart, enabling him to forgive his brothers. Joseph is a picture of Christ, suffering at the hands of evil people, knowing that it was God's ordained will for this to happen.

God never denies our prayer on account of our sin. He is gracious and willing to forgive. He grants us more than we either ask for or deserve. The forgiveness of sins, life, and salvation is infinitely more than we ever could have hoped for, being formerly slaves to sin. Although we deserve punishment on account of our sins, we now have the hope in Christ to be rescued from this world of sin.

Our heavenly Father also wants us to forgive and to do good to those who sin against us. "Just as we daily sin much against God, and yet He forgives everything through grace, so we, too, must ever forgive our neighbor who does us injury, violence, and wrong" (LC III 94). We cannot do this on our own. But the Holy Spirit works in our hearts through God's Word to give us the power to forgive others.

To hear an in-depth discussion of this Bible account, visit cph.org/podcast and listen to our Seeds of Faith podcast each week.

Lesson 10

Joseph Forgives His Brothers

Genesis 37:12–36; 45:1–15; 50:15–21

Connections

Bible Words
Be kind . . . forgiving one another, as God in Christ forgave you. Ephesians 4:32

Faith Word
forgive

Hymns and Songs
The King's Kids Are Prayin' (Director CD 9)
Lord Jesus, Think On Me (*LSB* 610)
The Lord's Prayer (*AGPS* 173 or Director CD 10)
What a Friend We Have in Jesus (*LSB* 770; Director CD 13)

Catechism
The Fifth Petition
We ask that our Father in heaven would for Christ's sake graciously forgive our sins. (Question 224)
Our heavenly Father wants us to forgive and to do good to those who sin against us. (Question 226)

Take-Home Point
God forgives me and wants me to forgive others.

1 Opening (15 minutes)

Welcome

To Prepare: Make copies of the Lesson 10 fair ticket (Director CD) and Resource Page 10, one per student. Have copies of "A Responsive Reading on Prayer" ready for use again and also a jump rope or other thin length of rope.

Sit behind the ticket window and greet students. Pass out Lesson 10 tickets.

Say **Welcome back to the Christian County Fair. Today, we will look at the Fifth Petition of the Lord's Prayer, "Forgive us our trespasses as we forgive those who trespass against us."**

Set out a thin rope along the length of the floor (not elevated). See if children can walk from one side to the other, using good balance. Suggest other challenges (e.g., walking backward, balancing something on their head).

Ask **The rope ladder game is frequently played at carnivals at fairs, but rarely do participants end up with a prize. Why does it seem so impossible to reach the top of the ladder? Who can explain how to play?** (The goal is to climb the ladder to reach the top and ring a bell without falling off.) **Who thinks they know the secret to winning?** (The climber must counterbalance, moving opposite arms and legs at the same time.)

Say **Carnival games seem impossible to win. In today's Bible account, Joseph seems to have an impossible task: to forgive his brothers. But it's no secret how to forgive; God tells us in His Word. Let's find out.**

Web Activity: Locate an appropriate video of someone successfully reaching the top of the rope ladder game.

MATERIALS NEEDED

1 Opening	2 God Speaks	3 We Live	4 Closing
Director CD Lesson 10 fair tickets (Director CD) Copies of "A Responsive Reading on Prayer" (Director CD or p. 12) Resource Page 10 Thin rope, at least several feet long	Bibles Student Leaflet 10	Bibles Activity Page 10 Plastic page protectors 8½ × 11-inch sheets of white cardstock (1 per child) Washi tape, various colors Rulers Dry-erase markers (1 per child) Medium-size pom-poms Small, self-adhesive glue circles	Director CD Lesson 10 fair ticket

Worship

Sing "The King's Kids Are Prayin'" (Director CD 9) or "Lord Jesus, Think On Me" (*LSB* 610). The songs emphasize God's forgiveness for us through Christ.

Invocation **In the name of the Father and of the Son and of the Holy Spirit. Amen.**

Hand out copies of "A Responsive Reading on Prayer" (Director CD or p. 12.) Use the reading together.

A "Fair"ly Good Clue to Learn a Fact about Prayer

Invite the students to take out their Lesson 10 fair ticket.

Ask **What "fair" ly good clue to learn about prayer do you see on your ticket?** (The milk bottle carnival game) **Who can tell me about the "knock over the milk bottle" game at the fair?** (A worker stacks the bottles, and a person tries to throw a ball at them and knock all of them over.) **Is the milk bottle game easy or difficult?** (Nearly impossible, like the ladder game)

Say **Difficult games help us learn about the Fifth Petition. We ask God to forgive us for our trespasses, which is another word for sins.**

Write the Faith Word, *forgive*, on the board.

Say **The Faith Word for this lesson is *forgive*. What does this word mean?** ("To overlook or forget a wrong that someone has done to you")

Say **The Fifth Petition not only talks about asking God to forgive us, but also reminds us that God expects us to forgive others and do good to them. Let's explore more about how God makes forgiveness possible.**

Prayer at the Fair Opening Devotion

Hand out Resource Page 10.

Say **As we check in on Emily and Zoey today, we find that the girls face a problem.** Ask volunteers to take turns reading out loud the devotion.

Ask **What problem arose between Emily and Zoey?** (They argued about what activity to do at the fair.) **How did the girls initially handle their disagreement?** (They were angry. They each went to do an activity alone.) **How do you know that the girls forgave each other?** (They admitted their selfish behavior to each other. They apologized, came back together as friends, and resolved the situation.)

Say **In today's Bible account, we will hear about forgiveness in a family of twelve brothers.**

Offering Encourage the students as they give their offerings. In response to God's mercy and forgiveness toward us, we give Him thanks.

Pray **Dear God, as we study Your Word today, help us to rejoice in Your forgiveness for us. Through the Holy Spirit at work in us, make us able to forgive even those who have really hurt us and to even do good to them. In Jesus' name we pray. Amen.**

Celebrate Recognize student birthdays, Baptism birthdays, and significant family events in your routine manner.

2 God Speaks (20 minutes)

Teacher Tip

You may want to provide some context for the story. Say, **Today's Bible account begins in the land of Canaan in the household of Jacob. His family were shepherds. Jacob had twelve sons; however, one was his favorite. This son was Joseph, his second-youngest child.**

God Teaches about Prayer

To Prepare: Have Bibles, Student Leaflet 10, and pencils ready for use.

Direct the students to the Blue-Ribbon Bible Stories arena. Hand out Bibles.

Ask **Jacob, also known as Israel, showed favoritism to his son Joseph by giving him a beautiful robe made of many different colors of cloth. Because Jacob favored Joseph, how do you think his brothers felt about him?** (They hated him. They were angry and filled with jealousy.)

Draw three stacked carnival milk bottles on the board, in a pyramid form. Write the words *hate*, *anger*, and *jealousy* inside, one word on each bottle.

Ask **The brothers had some serious problems.** Point to the words on the milk bottles. **And they just couldn't knock those unhealthy, sinful feelings out of their life, so the situation got worse.**

Locate Genesis 37. Invite a volunteer to read out loud Genesis 37:12–24.

Ask **What did Joseph's brothers do to him because of their hatred?** (They plotted to kill him and hide his body in an empty pit. Reuben convinced the others not to kill Joseph, but rather to throw him into the pit.)

Draw on the board three more milk bottles, stacked in another pyramid.

Ask **What sin did Joseph's brothers commit now?** (They were ready to murder Joseph.) Write the word *murder* inside one bottle.

Invite another volunteer to read out loud Genesis 37:25–36.

Ask **To whom did Joseph's brothers sell him?** (Ishmaelite/Midianite traders) **Where did they take Joseph?** (Egypt) **When he reached Egypt, to whom was Joseph resold?** (Potiphar, the captain of the guard for Pharaoh) **What sin did Joseph's brothers commit now?** (They were greedy to sell their brother as a slave to get money.) Write the word *greed* inside a bottle.

Ask **How did the brothers cover up their crime?** (They tore up Joseph's robe and made it look like Joseph had been killed by a wild animal.) **How did Jacob react when he saw Joseph's robe?** (He became very sad and mourned for days.) **What sin did Joseph's brothers commit now?** (They were thoughtless and hurt their father. They lied about what happened to Joseph.) Write *heartless*, *cruel*, *uncaring,* or *deceptive* inside the last bottle.

Say **There were some heavy problems weighing on this family that they couldn't get rid of.** Point to the milk bottles. **Does it seem like Joseph can do anything about the situation to make things better?** (No. Joseph probably felt fearful and helpless; there seemed to be no way out.)

Say **While he worked as a slave in Egypt, Joseph experienced many more hopeless situations. But no matter what happened to Joseph, the Bible tells us that "the Lord was with Joseph and showed him steadfast love"** (Genesis 39:21)**. While Joseph was in prison, God made it possible for him to inform Pharaoh that a famine was coming. So Egypt was able to store up food to prepare for this time when no food would grow.**

The Pharaoh gave Joseph the important position of distributing the

stored food. Eventually, Joseph's brothers came to Egypt to buy food from Joseph. Joseph recognized them, but they did not recognize him.

Help the students locate Genesis 45. Invite a volunteer to read verses 1–15.

Ask **What does the way Joseph now treats his brothers show? Did he seek revenge? What did God provide for Joseph?** (Joseph loved his brothers. He forgave them. He lavishly provided for them as he invited them and their families to come to Egypt even though they didn't deserve it.)

Fairly close to the milk bottles, draw six balls (circles). Inside one, write the word *generosity*, in another *care*, and in another *kindness*, representing the gifts God had blessed Joseph with to remove the wall of hostility.

Say **God provided Joseph with what he needed to knock down any bitterness that stood between him and his brothers.** Reread Genesis 45:7.

Ask **What did God lead Joseph to realize concerning why he was in Egypt?** (God used the sins of Joseph's brothers to save many lives during this time of famine, many years later.)

Invite a volunteer to read out loud Genesis 50:15–21.

Ask **After his father died, did Joseph change his mind about showing mercy to his brothers?** (No, but the brothers were afraid that Joseph would punish them now that Jacob was dead.) **Still troubled by their sin against Joseph, what did the brothers do?** (Asked for Joseph's forgiveness and even offered to be his slaves) **What were Joseph's actions toward his brothers after they asked for his forgiveness?** (He told his brothers not to be afraid. He promised to provide for them and their families.)

Write the words *love*, *forgiveness*, and *grace* inside the other three balls.

On his own, could Joseph have forgiven his brothers? (No; it was only through God at work in his life that he could forgive.) Point to the bottles. **These problems were too much for Joseph to handle on his own, but God gave him what he needed.** Draw arrows from one of the balls to one of the milk bottles, then erase the bottle. Repeat for the other balls and bottles.

Ask **God was there for Joseph all along, even when it seemed impossible to do something about the hurt that came his way. Let's reread verse 20. What did Joseph realize?** (God had worked good through all things.)

Review

Give the students time to find and circle each word in the word search. Then have them use all of the words to retell the Bible story to a friend.

Bible Words

Be kind . . . forgiving one another, as God in Christ forgave you. Ephesians 4:32

Locate the Bible Words on the student leaflet. Read them out loud together.

Ask **How did Joseph show the kind of forgiveness explained in the Bible Words?** (Through God's gift of forgiveness! Despite his brothers' sin against him, Joseph forgave them and provided food and care.) **And God doesn't treat us like we deserve; despite our sin, we have been forgiven.**

Write the Bible Words on the board. Have the students say them with you three times. Erase the word *kind* and replace it with a ball (circle), representing the gift of kindness God gave Joseph. Have students say the verse again, filling in the missing word. Now erase *forgiving* and *forgave*. Replace each word with a circle, God's gifts. Again, say the entire verse, including the missing words. Continue erasing the other words one by one, this time replacing them with blank lines instead of circles, until no words are left.

3 We Live (20 minutes)

Pray, Praise & Give Thanks

To Prepare: Make copies of Activity Page 10. Set out Bibles and pencils.

Have students gather their copy of the Lord's Prayer from their prayer pocket.

Say **Let's read out loud together the Fifth Petition of the Lord's Prayer: "Forgive us our trespasses as we forgive those who trespass against us." The Fifth Petition not only talks about asking God to forgive us, but also reminds us that God expects us to forgive others and do good to them.**

Teacher Tip

Note that you pay money to play a carnival game at the fair in the hope of winning a prize. God's grace is a free gift. We don't have to do something in order to receive His mercy. Jesus paid the price by giving His own life to save us from the punishment of sin. And our prize isn't just a cute stuffed animal, but life with God forever!

Locate Romans 6:23. Have the students read this verse with you out loud.

Ask **Does God have any obligation to forgive our sins?** (No. The price that needs to be paid to God for any sin is death.) Draw three new bottles on the board. Write one of the following words inside each: *sin*, *death*, and *devil*. Have the students copy the words on the bottles on their worksheet.

Ask **Instead of death, what does God offer to all sinners?** (Eternal life in Jesus) **God's salvation is a "free gift." There is nothing that we can do to earn it.** Draw three balls with one of the following words inside each circle: *forgiveness*, *life*, and *salvation*. Students fill in the balls on their page.

Say **Our Faith Word, *forgive,* means to completely wipe out what was wrong and to completely cancel the debt owed for sin.** Draw arrows from the three balls to the three bottles. Erase each bottle. **We deserve punishment because of our sins because we daily sin much, but because of Jesus, God forgives us. That undeserved mercy is called grace.**

Say **And the blessings continue. Not only do we pray that God would forgive our sins for Jesus' sake, but we also pray that God would help us to forgive others.**

Locate Colossians 3:13. Have the students read this verse with you out loud.

Say **How does God want us to treat others?** (Forgive them, as He has forgiven you) **How is this possible?** Read verses 14–17. (Only through Christ) **On our own, we can't forgive as we should, but through the Holy Spirit at work in our hearts through God's Word, Jesus helps us forgive others who have hurt us. He gave Joseph what he needed, and God gives *us* love, peace, and thankfulness, despite difficult situations and hurts.**

Direct the students to write inside the empty milk bottles three hurts that they've experienced that are hard to forgive (e.g., someone making a mean comment about them, someone not including them at recess or for a party).

Say **We need the Holy Spirit at work in our hearts because the two-way forgiveness involves one more step. Read Luke 6:27. How are we to treat those who hurt us?** (Do good to them!)

Point to Jesus' hand near the balls and remind the students that only through Christ are we able to forgive as He has freely forgiven us. Peace, love, and thankfulness in the midst of pain and hopelessness is a gift from God. Write those three words (*peace*, *love*, *forgiveness*) inside the balls. Have students place their Lord's Prayer back inside their prayer wheel pocket.

Craft—Dry-Erase Memo Boards

To Prepare: Provide a piece of white cardstock, a plastic page protector, a black dry-erase marker, a medium-size pom-pom, and one small self-adhesive glue circle for each child. Set out washi tape, scissors, and rulers.

Say **Today's Bible account was about forgiveness. When we forgive someone, we wipe clean their wrongs toward us and start new. Let's make a dry-erase memo board to remind us how God's forgiveness for us wipes away our sins and how God helps us to forgive others.**

Direct the students to slip the cardstock inside the page protector and trim off the hole punched edge, being careful to only cut off the white trim. Have students use rulers and scissors to measure and cut an 8-inch length of tape. Starting at the left-hand side of the open top end of the page protector, have the students place the tape along the top of the page protector and fold it over to close the top. *Note:* Keep a half-inch opening at the right-hand side of the page protector to hold the marker. Have each child place a glue circle to the top of a marker cap and add a pom-pom as an eraser.

4 Closing (5 minutes)

To Prepare: Have students bring their Lesson 10 ticket to the closing.

Sing "What a Friend We Have in Jesus (*LSB* 770; Director CD 13) or "Lord's Prayer" (*AGPS* 173:1–4) or "The Lord's Prayer" (Director CD 10).

Ask **Today's "fair"ly good clue about prayer on your ticket is a carnival game. What does it tell you about forgiveness?** (Even though we are sinful and "impossible" to love, Jesus loved us enough to die on the cross to grant us forgiveness. God helps us show that kind of love to others.)

Pray **Lord God, heavenly Father, we thank You for the love and forgiveness You give us through faith in Jesus. As we confess our sins to You, please wipe them away and give us clean hearts to love You and love others, even those who hurt us. We join together in the prayer that Jesus taught us.** (Conclude by praying the Lord's Prayer together.)

Direct the students to place their Lesson 10 ticket into their prayer wheel pocket. As each person leaves, say, **God forgives us and wants us to forgive others.**

Living the Faith

Encourage the children to use their dry-erase board to leave loving messages to family members this week, especially if someone in the family hurt them and are in need their forgiveness. Also encourage the students to do good to those who have hurt them by praying for them! God can use prayer to soften our hearts toward those who hurt us.

Snack

Homemade Lemonade

Through forgiveness, God can make something good out of a sour situation! Before class, mix 2 cups sugar and 2 cups water in a saucepan and heat, stirring until the sugar has dissolved. During class, cut lemons in half. Over a towel-protected surface, let each child poke the cut side of a lemon with a fork. While squeezing the lemon, move the fork up and down to juice the lemon. Use approximately 10 lemons to make 2 cups of fresh lemon juice. Combine the syrup mixture, strained lemon juice, and 1 gallon of water in a pitcher with ice and serve a homemade fair treat!

Forgive Us Our Trespasses as We Forgive Those Who Trespass against Us

Directions: Use the Bible verses to find sins and burdens, which are impossible for us to remove on our own. Write them inside the milk bottles. Then on the balls, write gifts that God has given us in Christ, making it possible to forgive.

1. Read Romans 6:23.

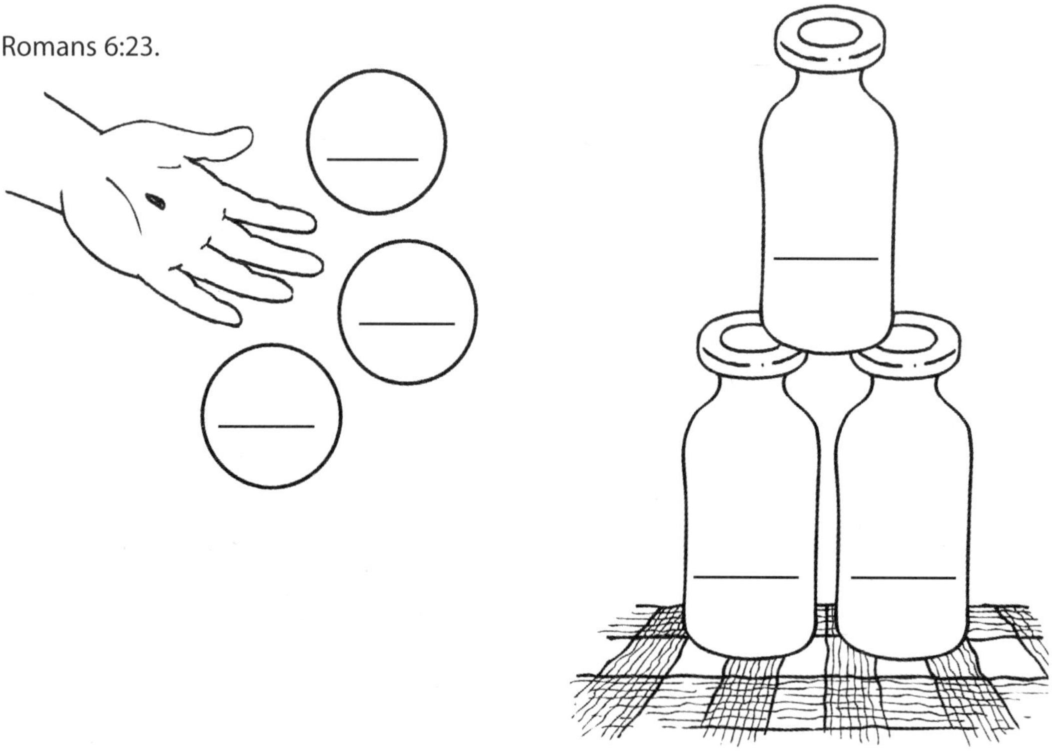

2. Read Colossians 3:13–17.

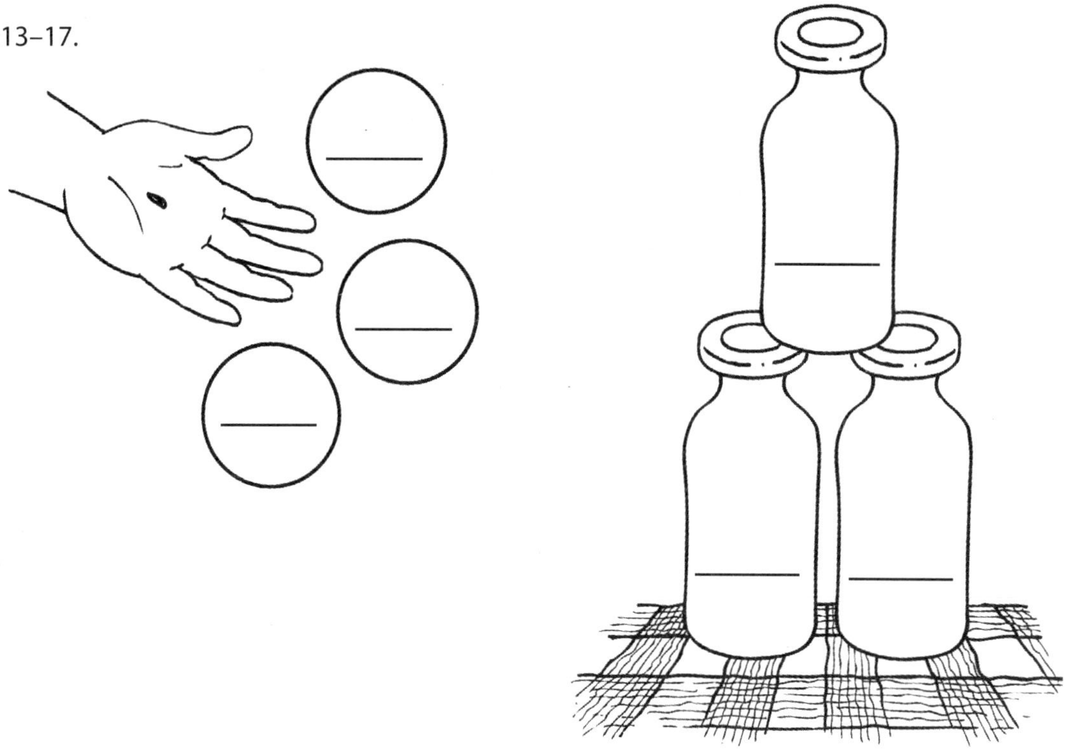

3. Read Luke 6:27.

Preparing the Lesson

The Temptation of Jesus

Matthew 4:1–11—God helps me resist temptation.

Key Point

Jesus resisted the temptations of the devil and kept God's Law for us because we cannot. Jesus strengthens us through His Word to resist temptation and assures us that He has won the victory over sin, death, and the devil for us.

Law/**Gospel**

Adam and Eve sinned by doubting God's Word and His goodness, and I do, too, when I don't trust God but give in to the devil's temptations. **Jesus, the new Adam, resisted temptations all the way to the cross, where He conquered Satan and sin forever for me. In Him, God forgives my sin, provides all that I need, and gives me strength to resist and overcome temptations.**

Context

At about the age of thirty, Jesus began His public ministry as Messiah and came to be baptized by John the Baptist in the Jordan. In this way, He fulfilled all righteousness. John confessed Him to be the Lamb of God who takes away the sin of the world. At His Baptism, Jesus took up the mantle of our salvation and from there proceeded to the cross to conquer sin, death, and the devil on our behalf.

Commentary

The Spirit led Jesus out into the wilderness to be tempted by the devil. This was a necessary second step for God in the flesh. He must first be baptized; then, He must face the devil head-to-head and resist temptation. Adam could not resist. He believed Satan's lies that God was holding something back from him. So Jesus, the second Adam, must face the tempter. Satan tempted the first Adam to be like God. He tempted the second Adam to go off and be God and leave the rebellious world to him.

After forty days of fasting, Jesus was hungry. It is at this time that the devil comes to tempt Him. First, he tempts Jesus with food: "If you are the Son of God," just do for Yourself what You did for the children of Israel in the desert. Make miraculous bread. Be God. But Jesus will not just be God. He took upon flesh to be true man too, so He could act in our place under the Law and fulfill it for us. He will not live by bread alone, but will rely upon God's Word for His sustenance.

So the devil takes Him to the Holy City, Jerusalem, to the pinnacle of the temple, and tempts Him with regard to God's Word. "All right, Jesus, if You want the Word of God, listen to its contradictions and cast Yourself off the temple, trusting what the Word of God says: 'on their hands they will bear You up.'" But Jesus will not allow seeming contradictions to obscure God's Word. Jesus answers, "You shall not put the Lord Your God to the test." Satan knows Scripture, but does not have faith. He chooses to quote from Psalm 91, which is actually written against him. In this messianic psalm, David prophetically wrote that the serpent would be trampled underfoot (91:13).

In the third temptation, the devil seeks to give Jesus what He's after without working for it. "I will give You" the kingdoms of the world. Just "fall down and worship me." It's as if he says, "Don't go to the cross, Jesus. Don't let Your heel be bruised for this rebellious people. Leave them to me." The devil wants Jesus to attend to the business of being God and to leave the world to him. But Jesus did not come to live at ease in this world. He came to win salvation for mankind by suffering and dying. The writer of the Book of Hebrews records Jesus' mission: "For because He Himself has suffered when tempted, He is able to help those who are being tempted" (2:18).

And so we pray in the Sixth Petition that God would give us strength to resist and overcome the devil, the world, and our sinful flesh, which would try to mislead us into false belief, despair, and other great sins. As God's children, we have the Holy Spirit, who works through God's Word to help us do this. But we still fail. Jesus, however, has won the victory over sin, death, and the devil for us. He resisted temptation so that He could be our Redeemer. He endured temptations, hardships, suffering, and even death because we are precious to Him. He is able to relate to us in all ways. He has suffered greater things than we have in this world, and He did it willingly. He took the punishments we deserved so that we could have the life that only He could give. He is true God and true man for us.

To hear an in-depth discussion of this Bible account, visit cph.org/podcast and listen to our Seeds of Faith podcast each week.

Lesson 11

The Temptation of Jesus

Matthew 4:1–11

Connections

Bible Words
Be watchful. Your adversary the devil prowls around like a roaring lion. . . . Resist him, firm in your faith. 1 Peter 5:8–9

Faith Word
temptation

Hymns and Songs
Lord Jesus, Think On Me (*LSB* 610)
Come, My Soul, with Every Care (*LSB* 779; Director CD 2)
The Lord's Prayer (*AGPS* 173 or Director CD 10)
What a Friend We Have in Jesus (*LSB* 770; Director CD 13)

Catechism
The Sixth Petition
The devil, the world, and our sinful nature try to mislead us into false belief, despair, and other great sins. (Question 229)
We ask our Father in heaven to give us strength to resist and overcome temptations. (Question 230)

Take-Home Point
God helps me resist temptation.

1 Opening (15 minutes)

Welcome

To Prepare: Before class, pour three different kinds of unwrapped, fragrant candy into three separate bowls. Make copies of the Lesson 11 fair ticket (Director CD) and Resource Page 11 (Teacher Guide), one per student. Provide copies of "A Responsive Reading on Prayer."

Sit behind the ticket window and greet students. Pass out Lesson 11 tickets.

Say **Welcome back to the Christian County Fair. Today, we will continue our study of the Lord's Prayer.**

Bring out the three bowls of candy on the serving tray. Walk back and forth in front of the students so they can see and smell the candy.

Say **This candy certainly looks and smells delicious, doesn't it? I bet it just makes your mouth water. But I'm sorry. You can't have any of it.**

Ask **How does it feel to see and smell the candy but not be able to eat any of it?** (Students share frustration.) **Are any of you tempted to come up and grab a piece? What are some of your favorite foods that you can hardly resist eating?** (Pizza, desserts, etc.) **If you saw and smelled these foods, but then were told you couldn't eat them, how might you react?** (You might want the forbidden foods even more or you might become frustrated, mad, or disappointed.)

Invite students to enjoy one or two pieces of candy.

Say **All around us are objects that we want, but may not be allowed to have. There are activities that we want to do that we may not be**

MATERIALS NEEDED

1 Opening	2 God Speaks	3 We Live	4 Closing
Director CD Lesson 11 fair tickets (Director CD) Three kinds of fragrant candy, like fruit or chocolate Three small bowls Serving tray Copies of "A Responsive Reading on Prayer" (Director CD or p. 12) Resource Page 11	Bibles Student Leaflet 11	Bibles Activity Page 11 Ballpoint pens or dull pencils Shield pattern (Director CD) White cardstock News and home-and-garden magazines Aluminum foil Stickers, rickrack, and glue (optional)	Director CD Lesson 11 fair tickets

allowed to participate in. Today, we will discuss how we can ask God to give us the strength to resist and overcome all things that can pull us away from Him. Right now, let's continue with song and prayer.

Worship

Sing "Lord Jesus, Think On Me" (*LSB* 610) or "Come, My Soul, with Every Care" (*LSB* 779; Director CD 2).

Invocation **In the name of the Father and of the Son and of the Holy Spirit. Amen.**

Hand out copies of "A Responsive Reading on Prayer" (Director CD or p. 12). Use the reading together.

A "Fair"ly Good Clue to Learn a Fact about Prayer

Invite the students to take out their Lesson 11 fair ticket.

Ask **What "fair"ly good clue to learn about prayer do you see on the ticket?** (A variety of fair foods—corn dogs, soda, and cotton candy.) **Imagine a tractor pulling these fair foods *toward* us.**

Write the Faith Word, *temptation*, on the board.

Ask **What does the word *temptation* mean?** (Let the students offer definitions.) **A temptation is something that you know you shouldn't have or that you know is wrong to do or want, yet you are pulled toward it. I just tempted you with some candy even though I told you that you couldn't have any of it. All kinds of things can pull us *away* from what we are supposed to do and *toward* what we are not supposed to do.**

Prayer at the Fair Opening Devotion

Hand out Resource Page 11.

Say **Today at the fair, Emily and Zoey are tempted by a delicious fair treat.** Ask volunteers to take turns reading out loud the devotion.

Ask **What happened because Emily and Zoey didn't resist the temptation to eat the funnel cake?** (They could barely eat their dinner. They were so full from all the food that they felt sick.) **According to the devotion, how are tractor pulls and temptation alike?** (Both involve pulling. In a tractor pull, people drive specially enhanced tractors to see how far they can pull heavy weights. When we are tempted, we are pulled toward doing something that we know is unwise, unhealthy, harmful, or sinful. We may resist for a while, but the temptation's pull often wins the "contest.")

Say **In today's Bible account, we will hear about a time when the devil tempted Jesus. Pay close attention to how Jesus fought against the devil and how Jesus gives us the strength to do so too.**

Offering Encourage the students as they give their offerings.

Pray **Lord Jesus, You are without sin. Help us to see that Your strength is what helps us resist the temptations of the devil, the world, and our sinful selves. In Your name we pray. Amen.**

Celebrate Recognize student birthdays, Baptism birthdays, and significant family events in your routine manner.

Web Activity: Locate a video showing a tractor pull. Use the key words "What is a tractor pull?" as you search for information. Preview all content.

2 God Speaks (20 minutes)

God Teaches about Prayer

To Prepare: Have Bibles, Student Leaflet 11, and pencils ready for use.

Direct the students to the Blue-Ribbon Bible Stories arena. Hand out Bibles. Help students locate Matthew 4:1. Read this verse out loud to the group.

Ask **Immediately after Jesus was baptized, the Holy Spirit led Him into the Judean wilderness. During this time, Jesus fasted. What does it mean to fast?** (Not to eat any food or to restrain from eating certain types of food for a specific period of time) **How did Jesus feel after fasting?** (Hungry!) **When you are hungry, how do you feel?** (Weak, disoriented, tired, crabby)

Say **Being hungry would have weakened Jesus' physical state. In this weakened state, Satan came to tempt Jesus.**

Direct the boys to read the even-numbered verses of Matthew 4:2–11. Direct the girls to read the odd-numbered verses. Tell each group to stand up whenever they are reading. Explain that you will stand with your back to the group and read the words of Satan as recorded in verses 3b, 6, and 9. After verse 11a is read by the girls, turn around.

Ask **How many days did Jesus spend there in the desert?** (Forty days and forty nights) **How many times did Satan tempt Jesus?** (Three) **With what weapon did Jesus fight against Satan and resist temptation?** (Holy Scripture) **What do these interactions tell us about Jesus?** (As true man, Jesus was tempted, yet He never sinned. As true God, Jesus had the power and authority to overcome temptation and triumph over Satan.)

Review

Hand out Student Leaflet 11. Have the students use their Bibles to complete the speech bubbles in the Search & Know activity on page 4.

Ask **How did Satan first tempt Jesus?** (Satan knew Jesus was hungry, so he tempted Jesus to turn some stones into bread.) **How did Jesus respond?** (He quoted God's Word from Deuteronomy 8:3. While Jesus could have done the miracle, He instead trusted in the Word of God to resist the devil.)

Ask **How did Satan next tempt Jesus?** (Satan tempted Jesus to throw Himself off of the top of the temple to test God to send His angels to save Him.) **How did Jesus respond?** (Jesus resisted Satan's tempting by quoting Moses' warning to Israel when they tried to test God [Exodus 17:2; Deuteronomy 6:16]. Jesus would have tested God's authority if He gave in.)

Ask **What was Satan's final temptation of Jesus?** (Satan tempted Jesus by telling Him he would give Him all the kingdoms of the world if Jesus would worship him.) **How did Jesus respond?** (Jesus resisted Satan's tempting by quoting Deuteronomy 6:13. The devil offered Jesus things in this world that are only God's to give. When Jesus tells Satan to "be gone" [Matthew 4:10], He shows His supreme authority as true God.)

Ask **What does this Bible account tell you about Jesus' two natures of true man and true God?** (Jesus is true man in that He was hungry and tempted by Satan's lies. Because of His encounter with Satan, Jesus understands how we feel when we are tempted to sin. Jesus is true God because He did not fall for Satan's lies; He never sinned. Jesus knew God's plan for Him was to save all people from their sins. Jesus resisted temptation so He could follow His Father's will. Jesus is stronger than anything or anyone.)

Bible Words

Be watchful. Your adversary the devil prowls around like a roaring lion. . . . Resist him, firm in your faith. 1 Peter 5:8–9

Locate the Bible Words on the student leaflet. Read them together.

Ask **What does the word *adversary* mean?** (An adversary is an opponent or enemy.) **What do these Bible Words tell you about the devil's power?** (It is something to be taken very seriously, and yet we know that God has defeated Satan through the death and resurrection of Jesus, and God promises us that with His help, we can resist the temptations of the devil, the world, and our sinful flesh.)

Ask **What does God's Word tell us to do concerning the devil?** (Be watchful and to resist Satan) **How do we resist Satan?** (We pray for and depend upon God's strength, found in His Word and Sacraments.)

Teach these actions to help students remember the verse.

Be watchful.	*(Shade eyes with hand as if watching.)*
Your adversary the devil	*(Raise fists as if ready to fight.)*
Prowls around like a roaring lion. . . .	*(Pace back and forth, pretending to roar.)*
Resist him,	*(Stand up straight, arms rigid.)*
Firm in your faith.	*(Stamp foot once; make a cross with index fingers.)*

3 We Live (20 minutes)

Pray, Praise & Give Thanks

To Prepare: Make copies of Activity Page 11. Gather Bibles and pencils or pens. Also gather some current news magazines and home-and-garden magazines. Provide scissors.

Direct students to get out their Lord's Prayer from the prayer wheel pocket.

Ask **By tempting Jesus, what was Satan trying to get Jesus to do?** (Forsake God and follow him instead) **Would Satan have been able to make good on the things he promised Jesus?** (No; his promises were lies.)

Say **Read John 8:44. How does Jesus know the devil is a murderer and the father of lies?** (Jesus is true God and knows everything. Jesus has existed with the Father and Holy Spirit from eternity. The triune God created the angels, which were all good angels until Satan and his followers rebelled against God and were thrown out of heaven. In Luke 10:18, Jesus told His disciples that He witnessed Satan falling like lightning from heaven.)

Ask **How is Satan a murderer?** (Satan can and does influence people to physically kill others. But worst of all, Satan kills people spiritually. Satan pulls and leads people away from God. His only mission is to separate people from God and from the saving faith found in Jesus Christ alone.) **What separates us from God from the time we are born?** (Our own sinful, selfish nature, which we inherit from Adam)

Hand out a news or home-and-garden magazine to pairs of students.

Say **Skim through the pages of the magazine you've been given. Find at least two examples of things that can separate us from God; cut them out. Anything that people hold as more important than God in their lives can separate us from Him.** Give the students a few minutes to do this.

Ask **What kind of things in the world did you find that can pull us away from God and toward our own sinful, selfish desires?** Let the children hold up their pictures; save them for later in the lesson. (These may include "good things" like money, jobs, family, friends, belongings, homes, hobbies, sports, and fame, and "bad things," like violence, conflict, natural disasters, disease, climate change, and political unrest.) Even good things can pull us away from God, because *we* like to decide what's good and desirable for ourselves instead of trusting in God's Word and *His* good plans for us. Tragedies can make us afraid and forget to trust in God's power and control.

Have students bring out their copies of the Lord's Prayer. Read out loud together the Sixth Petition, "And lead us not into temptation."

Say **The devil, the world, and our own sinful flesh work to lead us away from God. When we pray the Sixth Petition, we ask God to give us strength to resist and overcome temptations.**

Ask **Why can we trust in God's strength?** (Our Savior, Jesus, showed His almighty power and strength when through His death and resurrection, He defeated Satan and sin and eternal death's hold on us. When He returns to earth someday, Jesus will crush Satan for good. Everything will be good and perfect again, without sin to ruin our lives. There will be no more pain.)

Hand out Activity Page 11.

Say **On this page are some Scripture references to Bible truths we can call "temptation busters." Let's read these passages and summarize what they say about God's strength. Take turns locating and reading them and then writing a summary of ten words or fewer on the line.**

- **Romans 8:1:** Those who believe in Jesus are no longer condemned (deserving of the punishment of being eternally separated from God in hell).
- **Romans 8:31–32:** Our gracious God is for us!
- **Romans 8:35–39:** Nothing can separate us from God!
- **John 10:27–30:** Jesus will not let anyone take us from Him!
- **2 Corinthians 4:7–9:** God's power strengthens us!

Say **Jesus won the victory over sin, death, and the devil *for us*. He resisted temptation so that He could be our Redeemer, winning the ultimate tug-of-war contest between our enemies and us. Jesus endured temptations, hardship, suffering, and a horrible, painful death so that we wouldn't have to. Jesus even suffered separation from God as He hung on the cross so that we would never have to be separated from Him.**

Have students place their Lord's Prayer back inside their prayer wheel pocket.

Craft—Temptation Shields

To Prepare: On white cardstock, make copies of the shield pattern (Director CD). You will need the magazine pictures shown earlier, scissors, tape, aluminum foil, ballpoint pens (or dull pencils), and markers. Stickers, rickrack, and glue are optional. Students will also need Activity Page 11 again.

Say **God daily gives us the strength we need to resist temptation by the power of the Holy Spirit, who works through God's Word for us. In Jesus, we can stand firm in our faith. Let's make some temptation shields to remind us of the strength and protection for living that God gives.**

Hand out the shield patterns and scissors.

Say **Cut out the shield pattern, and then cover it in a sheet of foil. Tape the edges of the foil to the back of the shield. Then select one of the summarized Bible passages from Activity Page 11 to remind you that God is stronger than the devil's pull. Use a pen to gently write the summary on the middle of your shield, without poking through the foil. Then decorate the rest of your shield with the markers** (or other supplies)**.**

Teacher Tip

Have the students glue the rickrack trim around the edges of the shield *before* covering it with foil to create a textured design along the border. Show students how to make a handle for the back of the shield. Use strips of extra cardstock paper or scrunch a strip of foil to make it stronger. Tape the edges so the handle is vertical and children can grab it while holding their arm horizontally.

4 Closing (5 minutes)

To Prepare: Have ready the Lesson 11 fair tickets.

Sing "What a Friend We Have in Jesus" (*LSB* 770; Director CD 13) or "Lord's Prayer" (*AGPS* 173:1–5) or "The Lord's Prayer" (Director CD 10).

Bring out your Lesson 11 fair ticket.

Ask **Today's "fair"ly good clue about prayer is fair food. We imagined a tractor pulling these toward us. What does a tractor pull have to do with temptation?** (Temptations try to pull us away from God. God helps us to resist temptation. He is stronger than sin, death, and the devil.)

Pray **Dear God, You know that the devil, the world, and our own sinful nature try to pull us away from You with temptation and lies. Thank You for sending Jesus to resist all temptation and win the victory over sin for us, because we cannot. Help us, dear Father, to resist temptation as You give us strength through Your Word. And now together we pray the prayer Jesus taught us.** Conclude with the Lord's Prayer.

Direct the students to place their Lesson 11 ticket into their prayer wheel pocket. As each person leaves, say, **God helps us resist temptation.**

Snack

Corn Dogs

Serve a popular fair temptation. Thoroughly heat frozen corn dogs or mini corn dogs using a microwave or toaster oven. Provide ketchup and mustard. Consider how the hot dog is wrapped in the thick batter and how we are wrapped in the protection of God's powerful Word. When Satan throws temptations at us, our faith in Christ is our shield. Jesus provides us with all that we need to resist and overcome temptation.

Living the Faith

Challenge your students to make another fair treat at home—taffy! Instruct them to find a recipe online and work with an adult to cook the sugar. As they pull the cooked taffy for over thirty minutes, encourage them to think of how the devil relentlessly tries to pull us away from God. But thanks be to God, who gives us the victory through Christ! Challenge the children to share their taffy with a friend along with one of the Activity Page 11 verses.

And Lead Us Not into Temptation

Directions: Each of the Bible references below are from Bible truths that remind us that God's strength overcomes temptation. Locate and read each Bible passage. Then summarize each passage in ten words or fewer.

Romans 8:1

____

____

____

____

Romans 8:31–32

____

____

____

____

Romans 8:35–39

____

____

____

____

John 10:27–30

____

____

____

____

2 Corinthians 4:7–9

____

____

____

____

Lesson 12

Preparing the Lesson

Three Men in a Fiery Furnace

Daniel 3—God rescues me from every evil.

Key Point

God rescued the three faithful young men from the fiery furnace. God rescues us from harm and helps us endure the troubles that He allows to come into our lives.

Law/**Gospel**

The devil and evil, which have come into the world because of sin, cause hardship and troubles in my life. **In a world ruined by sin, God keeps me from harm and helps me to endure the troubles that He allows to come into my life, for the sake of Jesus, my brother and Redeemer, who rescued me from sin, death, and the devil and promises to be with me always.**

Context

Shadrach, Meshach, and Abednego were colleagues of Daniel. They were taken to Babylon as exiles from Israel and put into the service of King Nebuchadnezzar. They were educated in the language and ways of the people they served and advised the king in matters of state and policy. By the grace and direction of God, they excelled above their peers from other nations. This made their fellow advisers jealous. Before Daniel suffered under King Darius by being thrown into the lions' den, Shadrach, Meshach, and Abednego were persecuted by their peers who served King Nebuchadnezzar by being thrown into a furnace of fire.

Commentary

King Nebuchadnezzar made a golden image and commanded representatives from every province of Babylon to gather for its dedication. Babylon was the mightiest nation at this time (ca. 600 BC). They conquered all the nations around them, including Israel. The conquered nations served different gods and had various religions. It appears that King Nebuchadnezzar was trying to unite the nations under one religion, or at least to impose a state religion above other religions. He had representatives from every province at the dedication of his golden image. When they all bowed in worship to his gods, they were expressing allegiance to the Babylonian empire in mind, body, *and* spirit.

Most religions at this time allowed for other gods to be given due honor. However, the Jewish nation was monotheistic and did not allow room for the worship of other gods (Exodus 20:3ff). When Shadrach, Meshach, and Abednego heard the call to bow down to the golden image, they refused to fall down and worship it. Every other nation fell down and worshiped due to the threat of death in the fiery furnace. They alone refused. Certain Chaldeans reported this to the king, and Shadrach, Meshach, and Abednego were brought before Nebuchadnezzar. The king was furious. He commanded them to either fall down and worship his gods or be immediately cast into the furnace. He did not think any god could rescue them from that.

They answered him in a confession of faith. They said, "Our God whom we serve is able to deliver us from the furnace and from you. But even if He chooses not to, we will never serve your gods." After heating it seven times hotter than normal, the three men were thrown in. Yet they were not burned! The king was astonished and noticed that there were not just the three men he had thrown into the fire, but a fourth walking around with them. His observation was that the fourth person looked like a son of the gods.

It's also possible that "His angel" (v. 28) refers to one of God's heavenly angels, though "His angel" and "Angel of the Lord" in Scripture also often refer to a theophany (God appearing in human form). Whether it was the preincarnate Jesus or a heavenly angel, Shadrach, Meshach, and Abednego were protected from the fire. Their hair was not singed; their clothes did not burn or even smell like fire. The Lord had delivered them from the fire and the rage of the king. This divine intervention changed the king's heart toward Shadrach, Meshach, and Abednego and toward the God they served. He made a decree that no one could speak against the God of the Jews.

God, the true God alone, delivers from evil. He rescues from every evil of body and soul. This does not mean that we won't be persecuted or hurt by people who hate God. Thousands of Christians have suffered as martyrs, beginning with Stephen and continuing today. But any harm that comes to our body from persecution will not serve evil. It will serve to confess the true God who loves His people and brings them out of death into life eternal in Christ Jesus.

To hear an in-depth discussion of this Bible account, visit cph.org/podcast and listen to our Seeds of Faith podcast each week.

Lesson 12

Three Men in a Fiery Furnace

Daniel 3

Connections

Bible Words
The Lord will rescue me from every evil deed and bring me safely into His heavenly kingdom. 2 Timothy 4:18

Faith Word
deliver

Hymns and Songs
Children of the Heavenly Father (*LSB* 725; Director CD 1)

The Lord's Prayer (*AGPS* 173 or Director CD 10)

We Praise You, O God (*LSB* 785; Director CD 11)

What a Friend We Have in Jesus (*LSB* 770; Director CD 13)

Catechism
The Seventh Petition

The Lord keeps us from harm and helps us to endure the troubles that He allows to come into our lives. We want [God] to keep us faithful to Him and when we die to take us . . . to Himself in heaven. (Questions 232–233)

Take-Home Point
God rescues me from every evil.

1 Opening (15 minutes)

Welcome

To Prepare: Provide 16-ounce plastic cups; you will need six per child. Make copies of the Lesson 12 fair ticket (Director CD) and Resource Page 12, one per student. Have copies of "A Responsive Reading on Prayer" ready for use again.

Sit behind the ticket window and greet students. Pass out Lesson 12 tickets.

Say **Welcome back to the Christian County fair and to our Sunday School course, *Pray, Praise & Give Thanks: Jesus Teaches Us to Pray*. Today, we will focus on how God brings us through challenges in our lives.**

Bring out the plastic cups. Set them in small stacks on an empty table.

Say **At fairs, there are often challenging competitions. Let's have a challenge here at our classroom fair! For the next two minutes, practice stacking your six cups into a pyramid as fast as you can.**

Model how to stack the cups into a pyramid shape, all facing upside down. Place three on the bottom, two in the middle row with the open edges resting on the closed surface of the bottom row of cups, and one cup on the top.

Say **Think about how you set out the cups. Can you use both hands at the same time? What's the best order to stack the cups?** (Let one cup slide out, then right hand, left hand, right hand, left hand, top.) **Can anyone do it in less than ten seconds? five seconds?**

Use a clock, watch, or phone app to time the students. Encourage them along the way and recognize improvements in form.

MATERIALS NEEDED

1 Opening	2 God Speaks	3 We Live	4 Closing
Director CD Lesson 12 fair tickets (Director CD) 16-oz. plastic cups, 6 per child Copies of "A Responsive Reading on Prayer" (Director CD or p. 12) Resource Page 12	Bibles Student Leaflet 12 Hula-Hoop Extra cups (optional) Permanent marker (optional) Orange crepe paper (optional)	Activity Page 12 16-oz. plastic cups (1 each) 20-inch lengths of yarn or ribbon Clear packaging tape Button (or wooden bead or cork) (1 each) Fine-point black permanent markers Electrical or washi tape	Director CD Lesson 12 fair tickets Ten 16-oz. plastic cups (see Opening and Craft)

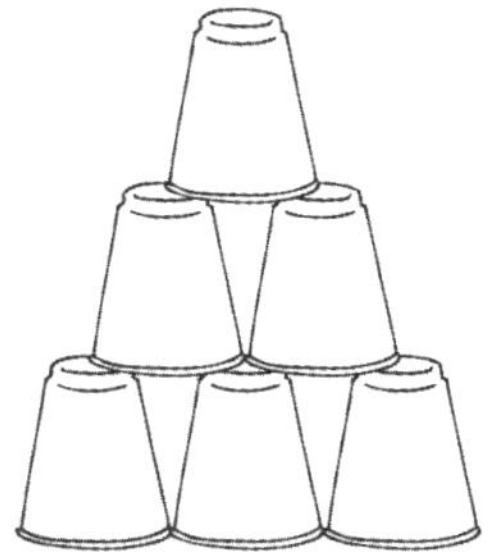

Say **That cup stack was a challenge! Today in our Bible lesson, we will meet three young men who faced a life or death challenge. We will discover how God rescued them from evil. Let's first continue our time at the fair with song and prayer.**

Web Activity: Locate an appropriate video showing speed cup stacking. Use the key words "cup stacking competition."

Worship

Sing "Children of the Heavenly Father" (*LSB* 725; Director CD 1) or "What a Friend We Have in Jesus" (*LSB* 770; Director CD 13). These songs emphasize the power, strength, and unending help Jesus gives us in times of need.

Invocation **In the name of the Father and of the Son and of the Holy Spirit. Amen.**

Hand out copies of "A Responsive Reading on Prayer" (Director CD or p. 12). Use the reading together.

A "Fair"ly Good Clue to Learn a Fact about Prayer

Invite the students to take out their Lesson 12 fair ticket.

Ask **What "fair"ly good clue to learn a fact about prayer do you see on today's fair ticket?** (A motorcycle and rider jumping through a ring of flames) **What dangers do you think are a part of a stunt like this one?** (Being burned by fire, crashing the motorcycle, scrapes, cuts, broken bones from a crash, even physical death)

Say **The ring of flames surround the motorcyclist. Dangers surround us. We pray that God keeps us from harm and helps us through trouble.**

Prayer at the Fair Opening Devotion

Hand out Resource Page 12.

Say **Emily and Zoey are still in the grandstand. Let's find out what happens after the tractor pull.** Ask volunteers to take turns reading the story.

Ask **How do you know that Flaming Frank trusted in God?** (He prayed both before and after his dangerous jump.)

Write the Faith Word, *deliver*, on the board.

Ask **After his jump, Frank thanked God for His deliverance. What does the Faith Word, *deliver*, mean?** (To rescue) **In what ways did God deliver Frank?** (God protected him from burns with the special protective gear God gave scientists the ability to develop. God gave Frank a trusty crew and skilled paramedics to help him. God protected Frank from serious injury.)

Say **Get ready for another flaming and dangerous incident in today's Bible account. Look for how God delivered those who were in danger.**

Offering Encourage the students as they give their offerings. Offerings give thanks to God for His protection.

Pray **Dear God, as we study Your Word, may the Holy Spirit strengthen our trust in Your care and power. Lead us to see Your work of deliverance in our lives. In Jesus' name we pray. Amen.**

Celebrate Recognize student birthdays, Baptism birthdays, and significant family events in your routine manner.

Teacher Tip

If time permits, discuss other potentially dangerous activities the children themselves might have seen at a fair (e.g., rodeos, car races, wild animal shows, scary rides).

2 God Speaks (20 minutes)

God Teaches about Prayer

To Prepare: Provide Bibles and pencils. If desired, make simple cup puppets for each character by using a permanent marker to draw faces on extra plastic cups turned upside down. Use the Hula-Hoop to represent the furnace.

Direct the students to the Bible story arena. Help students locate Daniel 3.

Say **Shadrach, Meshach, and Abednego were friends of Daniel. You will recall that we learned about Daniel in the very first Bible account that we studied this summer. Shadrach, Meshach, and Abednego were also taken to Babylon as exiles from Israel. These three young men were chosen by the Babylonian king, Nebuchadnezzar, to serve him as advisers. By God's grace, the three men did well in their jobs. However, this made the other advisers of the king jealous.**

Ask a volunteer to read out loud Daniel 3:1–7.

Ask **What did King Nebuchadnezzar build?** (A huge golden idol that was roughly ninety feet tall) **What did the king command all the people to do concerning the idol he built?** (Whenever the special music was played, everyone had to worship the idol.) **What was the punishment for those who did not follow the king's command?** (Being thrown to their death into a "burning fiery furnace")

Ask another volunteer to read out loud Daniel 3:8–15.

Ask **What did the king's jealous advisers tell him concerning Shadrach, Meshach, and Abednego?** (They would not bow down to the king's god.) **What was King Nebuchadnezzar's reaction to this news?** (He was "furious." He had the three men brought before him so he could personally ask them if what the advisers had told him was true.)

Invite another volunteer to read out loud Daniel 3:16–23.

Ask **What did Shadrach, Meshach, and Abednego tell King Nebuchadnezzar?** (Their God would deliver them from the king's fiery furnace.) **The three men added that even if God did not rescue them, they would still only serve the one true God. In saying that, what commandment did they follow?** (They followed the First Commandment, "You shall have no other gods before Me" [Exodus 20:3].)

Ask **Shadrach, Meshach, and Abednego's response made King Nebuchadnezzar even angrier. What did the king order?** (That the furnace be made seven times hotter than before and that Shadrach, Meshach, and Abednego be tied up while wearing all their clothing and then thrown into the furnace by men from Babylon's army. The fire was so hot that it killed the soldiers who threw the three men into the furnace.)

Invite a fourth volunteer to read out loud Daniel 3:24–30.

Say **When King Nebuchadnezzar looked into the furnace, he saw a fourth person walking around with the other three men. What did God do for Shadrach, Meshach, and Abednego as they faced death in the**

Teacher Tip

Many people who study the Bible believe that it was Jesus walking in the fire with Shadrach, Meshach, and Abednego. Other scholars believe this fourth person was one of God's angels. Whether this was Jesus or an angel, Shadrach, Meshach, and Abednego were protected in the fire.

furnace's fire? (God delivered them. He rescued them from death.) Point to the Faith Word, *deliver*, on the board. **God's deliverance for the three men was so complete that there was no evidence on them that they had ever even been anywhere near a fire. They didn't even smell like smoke!**

Ask **What new decree did King Nebuchadnezzar make after this miraculous rescue?** (That no one could speak out against the God of Shadrach, Meshach, and Abednego or they would be killed and their houses destroyed) **What else did the king do for the three men?** (Promoted them)

Review

Hand out Student Leaflet 12. Give students some time to fill in the rhyming words to complete the story facts in the Search & Know activity on page 4. Then review the answers together. **Answers:** 1. captivity; 2. demand; 3. tossed; 4. decree; 5. trust; 6. go; 7. four; 8. smoke; 9. saw; 10. way.

Bible Words

The Lord will rescue me from every evil deed and bring me safely into His heavenly kingdom. 2 Timothy 4:18

To Prepare: Have on hand a Hula-Hoop. As an option, decorate the Hula-Hoop with strips of orange construction or crepe-paper to represent fire.

Locate the Bible Words on the student leaflet. Read them out loud together.

Say **We pray that God would rescue us from evil and at the end of our lives on earth, take us to Himself in heaven, where we will live with Him forever in perfection. Evil does not exist in God's presence; He is holy.**

Divide the class into four groups. Direct each group to stand in a different corner of your classroom. Assign each group one of the verse parts:

The Lord will rescue me / from every evil deed / and bring me safely into / His heavenly kingdom.

As you stand in the center of the room holding the Hula-Hoop, point at each group one by one and have each group say its verse part in order. Have parts 1 and 2 stand in opposite corners and parts 3 and 4 stand in opposite corners of the room. As they say their part, have them walk (or jump) through the Hula-Hoop, and then turn around and walk back to their corner. Do this several times, a little faster each round.

3 We Live (20 minutes)

Pray, Praise & Give Thanks

To Prepare: Make copies of Activity Page 12. Have pencils ready.

Direct students to get out their Lord's Prayer from the prayer wheel pocket. When students are settled, read out loud together the Seventh Petition, "But deliver us from evil." Point to the word *deliver* on the board.

Ask **What does the word *deliver* mean?** (To rescue) **From what evil did God deliver Shadrach, Meshach, and Abednego?** (The deadly fire in the furnace) **From what deadly fire has God delivered you?** (The deadly fire of eternal death in hell) **How?** (Jesus' death and resurrection)

Say **Shadrach, Meshach, and Abednego knew that even if God did not choose to save them physically from the fire in the furnace, He would save them spiritually from eternal death. We, too, can trust that God rescues from every evil of body and soul.**

Ask **Because God has rescued you from sin, death, and Satan through faith in Jesus, what do you know will happen to you, even if you physically die?** (God will take us to heaven to live with Him there forever.)

Say **Sin has ruined our world. Until Jesus returns to earth someday, evil is a sad reality in our lives. When we pray in the Lord's Prayer, "but deliver us from evil," we ask God to keep us from harm and to help us make it through the troubles of this world.**

God does not *cause* bad things because God is only good. But God *allows* bad things to happen. He can bring good through them. God uses troubles and hardships to draw us closer to Him in faith. God uses difficult times as opportunities for us to witness our faith in Jesus to others. Finally, one day we will be with God in heaven, away from the troubles of this life. This is the ultimate deliverance from evil.

Ask **Why can we trust that God will deliver us from evil?** (In His Word, God promises to do this for us. God never breaks a promise. God has already rescued us from sin, death, and Satan by giving up His Son to die on the cross for our sins. Jesus' resurrection proves His power over death.)

Hand out Activity Page 12. Ask a volunteer to read out loud the directions at the top of the page. Emphasize that there is evil that affects all areas of our lives: body, soul, reputation, and possessions. Discuss what might be happening. Which Bible verse might bring comfort in each situation?

- Daniel's grandma is gravely ill. Daniel prays for God to heal her. But his grandma's condition continues to worsen. "Doesn't God hear my prayers?" wonders Daniel.
- Every day when he walks home from school, Jacob sees drug dealers throughout his neighborhood. He thinks his big brother, Jordan, might have been talking with them when he skipped church last Sunday.
- Several girls in Ava's class make fun of her because she prays each day in the lunchroom before she eats her lunch.
- Maddie's dad lost his job. Her family faces losing their home. Maddie worries they might have to live in a homeless shelter.

Answers: Any of the Bible verses can be used in every situation, but as students suggest certain ones, ask them to explain why.

Have students place their Lord's Prayer inside their prayer wheel pocket.

Craft—God Rescues Us Cup Activity

To Prepare: Provide a 16-ounce plastic cup and a button (or large wooden barrel bead or cork) for each student. Cut a 20-inch length of yarn for each student. You will also need several fine-point black permanent markers, clear packaging tape, scissors, and various colors and designs of electrical tape or washi tape.

Say **God rescues us from every evil. Let's make an activity that reminds us that God promises to deliver us from harm and troubles.**

Give each student a cup. Provide various kinds of tape for students to use to decorate the outside of their cup. Next, give each person a button and a piece of the precut ribbon or yarn. Students use a small piece of clear packaging tape to attach the button to one end of the ribbon and attach another small piece of tape to the other end of the ribbon. Have them press this end of the ribbon firmly in place on the outside bottom of the cup. Have the students draw a smiley face with permanent marker on the button to represent themselves (or add a smiley face sticker).

Demonstrate how to do the cup activity. As you hold the cup in one hand, gently swing the ribbon in front of the cup and try to catch the button inside the cup. Each time you catch the cork or button say, **God rescues me from every evil.** Invite the students to try the activity themselves.

Snack

Nachos, Cheese, and Salsa

Heat up some spicy hot (and mild) cheese dip in a microwave. Also set out some spicy hot (and mild) salsa. Place a small ladle in each. Put some tortilla chips on a small paper plate for each student. Let them spoon some cheese and salsa onto their plate for dipping their chips. Who can "take the heat"? When situations intensify, God is there by our side!

4 Closing (5 minutes)

To Prepare: Have students bring their Lesson 12 fair ticket with them to the closing. Also bring ten plastic cups.

Sing "We Praise You, O God" (*LSB* 785; Director CD 11), or review "Lord's Prayer" (*AGPS* 173) or "The Lord's Prayer" (Director CD 10).

Bring out your Lesson 12 fair ticket.

Ask **Today's "fair"ly good clue about prayer shows a motorcyclist jumping through a ring of fire. What does that have to do with our prayer petition, "But deliver us from evil"?** (Through Jesus' death and resurrection, He has defeated evil for us. We pray for God's continued protection from danger and evil in this world until He safely brings us to heaven.)

Have several volunteers help you to make a cross on the floor of the worship area using the plastic cups. Set down six cups to make the vertical post. Add two cups to each side of the vertical post to make the crossbar. Form a circle around the cross as you pray the closing prayer.

Pray **Heavenly Father, through the death and resurrection of Your Son, Jesus, You have rescued us from sin, death, and Satan. Be with us every day as we face troubles and dangers in this world. By the power of the Holy Spirit, keep our faith strong. One day, bring me safely into Your heavenly kingdom. And now we pray together the prayer that Jesus taught us.** Pray together the Lord's Prayer.

Direct the students to place their Lesson 12 fair ticket into their prayer wheel pocket. As each person leaves, say, **God rescues us from every evil.**

Living the Faith

Encourage the students to memorize one or more of the Bible verses on Activity Page 12 as reassurances for them of God's rescue through their own difficult times. Suggest they share these Scripture truths with others in need.

But Deliver Us from Evil

Directions: On the flames below are dangerous situations. Talk about each situation and read the reassuring truths from God's Word from inside the flaming ring. If you could talk to the people in each situation, which of these truths would you share to help them in their time of trouble? Draw a line from the flame to the verse.

When you walk through fire you shall not be burned, and the flame shall not consume you. **Isaiah 43:2**

+ The LORD will keep you from all evil; He will keep your life. The LORD will keep your going out and your coming in from this time forth and forevermore. **Psalm 121:7–8**
+ But the Lord is faithful. He will establish you and guard you against the evil one. **2 Thessalonians 3:3**
+ [God says,] "And call upon Me in the day of trouble; I will deliver you, and you shall glorify Me." **Psalm 50:15**
+ Grace to you and peace from God our Father and the Lord Jesus Christ, who gave Himself for our sins to deliver us from the present evil age, according to the will of our God and Father. **Galatians 1:3–4**

Lesson 13

Preparing the Lesson

The Saints in Heaven

Revelation 19:1–10—God has power to answer my prayers.

Key Point

The saints in heaven praise God for His power and glory and wisdom. God, who is all powerful, loving, and wise, will answer our prayers as He has promised.

Law/**Gospel**

The prince of this world seeks to corrupt me by sin, suffering, and death and causes me to doubt God's love and ability to answer my prayers. **God alone is the King who has all good gifts in His control and the power to grant my petitions. He will answer my prayers for the sake of Jesus, the Lamb who was slain in payment for my sins, so I can live joyously in heaven with Him forever.**

Context

God gave a special revelation to John in order to show him the things that must soon take place. An angel caught John up into heaven and gave him a glimpse of the joy to come in heaven. The purpose for the Book of Revelation is to give comfort to the Christian congregations who suffer under the hand of sin and persecution. Jesus is portrayed as the Lamb sitting upon His throne, receiving the prayers and praises of all the angels, saints, and elders in heaven. He alone is the Savior of all, the one who defeated the beast, brings the new heaven and new earth, and will come again.

Commentary

The voice of the multitude in heaven is the voice of all the people who have believed that Jesus is their Lord and Savior, from the beginning of the world until its end. It's the voice of victory. The Lamb has been slain for the sins of the world, but He is not dead. He lives and has ascended into heaven to prepare a place for all believers. He sits triumphantly upon His throne, worshiped by saints and angels.

John records for us the hymns sung by the saints in heaven. Singing is a divine activity. Song did not originate in this world. The words of these songs come straight from heaven, revealed by God Himself. The angels sing. The saints in heaven sing. And the song echoes in Christian churches throughout the world. The content of these hymns of praise and victory gives us insight into what's important to God and to the Church Triumphant.

Hallelujah is the Hebrew word that means "praise the Lord." Praise is the theme of these songs, and each of them expounds upon the reason for this praise.

The first song praises the salvation, glory, and power that belong to God because of His judgments. He has pronounced condemnation upon the devil and his evil angels who corrupted the earth. He has pronounced liberty to His servants, avenging their blood that was spilled. This twofold judgment condemns those who do not believe in the Lamb to eternal death, but proclaims forgiveness and eternal life to those who believe and are baptized (John 16:8).

The second song builds on the first, eliciting a response from the elders and the beasts confirming what they just sang. The voice from the throne calls for more praise and fear from the congregation of the saints. And they respond.

The third song praises God for His mighty reign. He is the all-powerful King. His kingdom is everlasting. He prepares as His Bride the Church universal, all those who believe in Jesus as their Lord and Savior. What reassurance this gives: God who has all power loves us so much that He sent Jesus to redeem us and answers all our prayers!

The wedding in the text is a picture of the future event when Christ comes again to inaugurate the new heaven and the new earth. It's the final day that initiates eternity. It's the day when all the souls of the saints are reunited with their bodies in the long-awaited reunion in heaven. The invitation has been sent through the prophets, evangelists, and preachers to the world (Luke 14:23) . The banquet begins!

The Bride, all those who believe in Him, is clothed in the bright, pure linen robe of her Bridegroom, washed in the blood of the Lamb. Christ's justification is combined with the sanctification of His saints on the Last Day. His life and works are attributed to them (Matthew 25:34–39).

The Lamb, His Word, and salvation are all worthy of the praise of the Church Triumphant and the Church Militant. It is the underlying component in all hymns of praise. The Church on earth continues to echo heavenly praises as long as this world remains. Soon, we will be caught up in this heavenly chorus!

To hear an in-depth discussion of this Bible account, visit cph.org/podcast and listen to our Seeds of Faith podcast each week.

Lesson 13

The Saints in Heaven

Revelation 19:1–10

Connections

Bible Words
Salvation and glory and power belong to our God. Revelation 19:1

Faith Word
hallelujah

Hymns and Songs
This Is the Feast (*LSB* 155; *AGPS* 242)

We Praise You, O God (*LSB* 785; Director CD 11)

The Lord's Prayer (*AGPS* 173 or Director CD 10)

How Majestic Is Your Name (*AGPS* 122)

Catechism
Conclusion and Amen

Amen means "so shall it be" and emphasizes that God . . . will hear our prayers and answer them. [God] alone is the King who has all good gifts in His control. He alone has the power to grant our petitions. He has all glory and is worthy of our praise. (Questions 234–235)

Take-Home Point
God has power to answer my prayers.

1 Opening (15 minutes)

Welcome

To Prepare: Before class, place a hymnal for each student on a table in your classroom. Make copies of the Lesson 13 fair ticket (Director CD). Have copies of "A Responsive Reading on Prayer" ready for use again today.

Sit behind the ticket window and greet students. Pass out Lesson 13 tickets.

Say **Welcome back to the Christian County Fair and to our Sunday School course, *Pray, Praise & Give Thanks: Jesus Teaches Us to Pray.* Today is closing day at our fair. Get ready for a day of praise to our triune God as we focus on the conclusion of the Lord's Prayer.**

Direct each student to take a hymnal.

Say **Many of the hymns in our hymnals and songbooks contain words that praise God for who He is and for what He does for us. Skim through the hymnal and shout out any words of praise to God that you find.**

As the students call out words of praise, write them on the board. Your list should include such words as *great, mighty, almighty, wonderful, powerful, glory, glorious, victory, king, kingdom, throne, triumphant, joyful, holy, blessed, adoration, celebration*. If *alleluia* and/or *hallelujah* are mentioned, add them to the list. You will call special attention to this word later in the lesson.

Say **These words are in these hymns because God is almighty! Today, we will learn that God has power to answer our prayers and that He alone**

MATERIALS NEEDED

1 Opening	2 God Speaks	3 We Live	4 Closing
Director CD Hymnals (*LSB* or *AGPS*, 1 each) Lesson 13 fair tickets (Director CD) Copies of "A Responsive Reading on Prayer" (Director CD or p. 12)	Bibles Student Leaflet 13	Bibles Activity Page 13 3 × 5-foot piece of banner paper Newspaper or plastic table cover Brightly colored skeins of yarn Scarves and rhythm instruments (optional)	Director CD Lessons 1–13 fair tickets (from students' prayer wheel pockets in worship area)

is worthy of our praise. Let's continue our time at the fair with song and prayer. Please take a hymnal with you.

Worship

Sing "This Is the Feast" (*LSB* 155; *AGPS* 242) or "We Praise You, O God" (*LSB* 785; Director CD 11).

Invocation **In the name of the Father and of the Son and of the Holy Spirit. Amen.**

Hand out copies of "A Responsive Reading on Prayer" (Director CD or p. 12). Use the reading together.

A "Fair"ly Good Clue to Learn a Fact about Prayer

Invite the students to take out their Lesson 13 fair ticket.

Ask **What "fair"ly good clue to learn about prayer do you see on today's fair ticket?** (An exploding firework) **What is the usual reason why fireworks are displayed?** (For celebrations) **What are some events where you've seen fireworks displayed?** (Independence Day, New Year's Eve, after baseball games, etc.)

Say **Fireworks are a glorious way to celebrate joyful events. At many county and state fairs, fireworks are a part of the festivities. Today, we'll celebrate our joy that God answers prayers. We'll celebrate how loving, wise, and all-powerful He is.**

Fireworks are often used to celebrate the successful end of a game, concert, or fair. We end each prayer with a powerful "boom"! The word *amen* is used to communicate a successful petition: God has certainly heard our prayer and there is no doubt He has the power and ability to answer our prayer. The power behind fireworks is gunpowder and sophisticated launching systems. The power behind prayer is the person of God! For Jesus' sake and in His name we can confidently pray.

Web Activity: Locate information about how fireworks are made, or watch an appropriate short video of a fireworks display.

Prayer at the Fair Opening Devotion

There is no prepared devotion for today. Have the students discuss how they think the story ends, or give them time to act out the final evening of the fair through role play.

Say **You'll remember that last time, Emily and Zoey saw an exciting daredevil motorcyclist, Flaming Frank. I wonder what happened next while they were at the grandstand. What do you think might be the final event at a county or state fair?** (Fireworks display)

Ask volunteers to take the role of Dad, Mom, Emily, and Zoey to develop their own closing devotion: "At the Fair: Explosions of Praise." If no students volunteer, discuss what the characters might have thought about during the show or give students time to write or draw their ideas. Encourage them to include a devotional thought about how the fireworks make them think of God (e.g., fireworks can remind us of the bright sky and the light of heaven when Jesus will someday return, fireworks can make us think of a reason why God deserves our thanks and praise).

Say **Our Bible account today focuses on God's power to answer our prayers. In it, we'll find out what God revealed to the apostle John about Himself, our all-powerful, all-wise, and all-loving God.**

Offering Encourage the students as they give their offerings. Offerings give thanks to God for all of His blessings, including answering our prayers.

Pray **Dear God, as we study Your Word today, fill our hearts with praise and love for You. We pray that You would not only increase our understanding of who You are, but also increase our trust in who You are—the only one who can answer our prayers. In Jesus' name we pray. Amen.**

Celebrate Recognize student birthdays, Baptism birthdays, and significant family events in your routine manner.

2 God Speaks (20 minutes)

God Teaches about Prayer

To Prepare: Have Bibles, pencils, and Student Leaflet 13 ready.

Direct the students to the Blue-Ribbon Bible Stories arena. Hand out Bibles and help students locate Revelation 19.

Say **In the Book of Revelation, the apostle John, who was one of Jesus' disciples, tells of the special vision of heaven that God gave him. John was given a special look at the joy to come for all believers when they reach their heavenly home. The vision of John that we are about to read tells of all the saints or believers who are in heaven and how they and other special heavenly creatures praise God and honor Him. In this reading, we also get a glimpse of God's power over all things in heaven and on earth.**

Invite the students to follow along in their Bibles as you read verses 1–5.

Ask **What is the word beginning with the letter *H* that is repeated several times in the verses I just read?** (Hallelujah)

Circle the Faith Word, *hallelujah,* on the word list that you compiled in the Opening time of today's lesson. If it's not on your list, write it on the board.

Say **The word *hallelujah* means "praise the Lord." This Faith Word is found at the beginning of each of the praise songs in the first ten verses of this chapter of Revelation.**

Ask **According to these verses, why do we praise God?** (Because salvation, glory, and power belong to Him. God alone has the power to judge. God has condemned the devil and the evil angels who ruined the earth. God forgives and saves those who believe in Jesus as their Lord and Savior.) **According to verse 5, who is to praise God?** (All God's servants, those in heaven and those on earth, are to praise Him.)

Invite the students to follow along in their Bibles as you read verses 6–8.

Say **This song praises God for His mighty reign. God is King. He is all-powerful. The "bride" mentioned in these verses is God's Church—all**

who believe in Jesus as their Lord and Savior. Our all-powerful God loves us so much that He sent the Lamb, Jesus, to save us! What great news! When Jesus returns someday, the souls of all believers who have died will be reunited with bodies that have been made new and perfect by Jesus. New, perfect bodies will also be given to all believers still alive on earth. Then all believers will join together in heaven to praise God and enjoy the marriage feast of Jesus to His Bride, the Church.

Invite students to follow along in their Bibles as you read verses 9–10.

Ask **John was so overwhelmed by all that he saw that he fell down and wanted to worship the angel who had taken him to see the vision of heaven. But what did the angel tell John?** (To "worship God." The angel wanted John to know that only God deserves the praise and glory for all that we are and have.)

Web Activity: Locate an appropriate video of the "Hallelujah Chorus" from Handel's *Messiah* oratorio. Listen for the text of Revelation 19:6 (and 16). Or find a video of "Ode to Joy flash mob" from Beethoven's Ninth Symphony. Follow along with the words to the hymn "Joyful, Joyful We Adore Thee" (*LSB* 803). Imagine yourself in the heavenly chorus!

Review

Hand out Student Leaflet 13. Work together as a class to match the phrases to complete the sentences in the Search & Know activity on page 4. **Answers:** 1. d; 2. c; 3. a; 4. b; 5. f; 6. e; 7. g.

Bible Words

Salvation and glory and power belong to our God. Revelation 19:1

Locate the Bible Words on the student leaflet. Read them out loud together.

Say **John heard these words when God allowed him to see a vision of believers rejoicing in heaven. The words are a cheer of victory to Jesus, our Lord and Savior. Listen carefully as I cheer the words of this verse.**

Sal-VA-tion and GLO-ry and POW-er (*clap, clap*)

BE-long TO our GOD. (*clap, clap*)

Repeat the cheer over and over as you invite the students to say it with you. Continue until the students know it well.

3 We Live (20 minutes)

Pray, Praise & Give Thanks

To Prepare: Make copies of Activity Page 13. Provide Bibles and pencils.

Direct students to get out their copy of the Lord's Prayer from their prayer wheel pocket. Read out loud together the Conclusion of the prayer, "For Thine is the kingdom and the power and the glory forever and ever. Amen."

Say **In the Bible account we read earlier from the Book of Revelation, God gives us a glimpse of heaven. In this look at heaven, we see the believers there proclaiming that God alone has power and glory.**

We see people praising God for who He is and for what He has done. When we pray the Conclusion to the Lord's Prayer, we are telling God that we believe He has power to answer our prayers.

Ask **What is the last word we pray in every prayer, including the Lord's Prayer?** (Amen) **The word *amen* means "so shall it be." The word *amen* draws attention to the fact that God will hear our prayers and will answer them as He has promised to do.**

Ask **How do we know God is able to answer our prayers?** (He alone is the King of all. God, our King, has all good gifts under His control. God alone has the power to grant the requests we pray to Him. God alone has all the glory and is worthy of our praise.)

Hand out Activity Page 13. Ask a volunteer to read the directions. Assign each student one of the Bible references listed on the page. Give students several minutes to locate and read their verse and write down one or more praise words to God that are found in it. As you call on students to reveal their answers, encourage students to write them in (over the top of) the additional exploding firework drawings on the page.

Answers: Psalm 113:4–5: unique, glorious, above all or supreme; **1 Timothy 1:17:** King, immortal, invisible, only God; **Isaiah 6:3:** holy, glorious; **Psalm 118:1:** good, enduring, loving; **1 John 4:8:** love; **Psalm 147:5:** great, powerful, wise; **Deuteronomy 32:4:** Rock, perfect, just, faithful, sinless, upright; **Malachi 3:6:** unchanging; **Psalm 103:13:** compassionate, Father; **Psalm 117:2:** stead-fast, faithful, loving, eternal.

Craft—Hallelujah Banner

To Prepare: Cut at least a 3 × 5-foot piece of butcher paper or bulletin board background paper. (Make the banner long enough so each student can have a section of it to work on at the same time.) If your paper is thin, cover the work area with newspaper or plastic table covering so that markers do not bleed through and stain the table. Provide pencils, markers, glue, scissors, and many different skeins of brightly colored yarn. Scarves and rhythm instruments are optional. Have students bring Activity Page 13 with them for reference.

Ask **Our Faith Word for this lesson is *hallelujah*. What does this word mean?** ("Praise the Lord")

Say **Let's make a hallelujah banner to praise God.** In the center of the banner, print and decorate the Faith Word, *hallelujah*. Give each student time to glue pieces of colorful yarn onto the banner to look like firework bursts surrounding the Faith Word. Start with a cross shape in the middle; then add other pieces trailing off the center. Curving the yarn strips can make it look more realistic. Suggest first making the entire firework design with the glue and then pressing the yarn strips on top. Also suggest using at least seven or eight strips of yarn for each burst.

If time permits, include on the banner many of the other praise words we discovered earlier in the hymns we sing, as well as those from the Bible that you discovered and wrote on Activity Page 13. Add Christian symbols and lots of bright colors.

We will display this banner in the (Sunday School hallway, Fellowship Hall, church narthex, other location) **when it's finished.**

Another option is to have two students hold the banner, one on each side, and lead the group in a march around the church, using a predetermined route that will not surprise or disturb any other classes. Give the other students rhythm instruments so the "band" can perform a song/hymn of praise, as bands sometimes march through the streets of a fair. (Or instead of a hymn of praise, a popular marching song that reminds us of heaven is "When the Saints Go Marching In.") Older students may want to act as a "color guard" group that marches in front of the band. Give them time to work on developing choreography for a very simple worship flag waving routine, using scarves or squares of other light fabric.

Web Activity: To inspire older students attempting to choreograph a short routine, locate an appropriate video that shows dancers waving worship flags. Search using the key words "worship flag dance." If you use the song "When the Saints Go Marching In," show a jazz band performance of it.

Teacher Tip

If you plan to march with the banner, communicate in advance, and practice the performance in advance. Plan the parade route ahead of time, so the other children or adults can look forward to you coming, or invite them to watch your performance in the last part of the Bible study time.

4 Closing (5 minutes)

To Prepare: Help students remove their prayer wheel pocket from the Ferris wheel and bring it with them with all their fair tickets (1–13) as they are seated for closing. Have a fair ticket from every lesson available for your use.

Sing "How Majestic Is Your Name (*AGPS* 122), or close with a familiar song such as "Lord's Prayer" (*AGPS* 173) or "The Lord's Prayer" (Director CD 10).

Bring out all your fair tickets in order from 1–13.

Say **Here at *Pray, Praise & Give Thanks*, we've had thirteen "fair"ly good clues about prayer. Let's take a moment to review them now.**

Briefly show each fair ticket. Invite students to state what each clue taught them about prayer. Then have everyone take out the Lesson 13 ticket.

Ask **Today's "fair"ly good clue about prayer is an exploding firework. What does this clue tell us about the Conclusion of the Lord's Prayer?** (It reminds us that we celebrate how God alone has the power to do all things for us, including answer our prayers. We "launch" our prayers to heaven, and boom! It shall be so; God will answer them in the way He knows is best, as He has promised.)

Pray **Lord God, salvation and glory and power belong to You. Thank You for hearing and answering all our prayers and for all that You do for us as our Lord and Savior. May we praise You forever for all Your goodness to us. And now we pray together the Lord's Prayer.** (Pray together, ending loudly on the Conclusion.)

As the students leave, have them take their fair tickets, their copy of the Lord's Prayer, and any craft projects they may have made throughout the course. As each person leaves, say, **God has power to answer our prayers.**

Snack

Cotton Candy

Purchase several bags of colorful premade cotton candy for the students to enjoy. If you want to go all out, rent a cotton candy machine and supplies from a party supply store and make your own. Use it outdoors in an open area to avoid cleanup. The puffy candy resembles clouds. Jesus ascended in the clouds and will someday return in glory in the clouds to take all believers to Himself in heaven.

Living the Faith

Encourage the students to show someone at home their fair tickets. Challenge them to explain the meaning of the clue on each ticket and how it relates to our prayers to God.

For Thine Is the Kingdom and the Power and the Glory Forever and Ever. Amen.

Directions: Locate and read each Bible verse referenced below. Inside the exploding fireworks, write praise words to God based on each verse, one word per firework.

Psalm 113:4–5

1 Timothy 1:17

Isaiah 6:3

Psalm 118:1

1 John 4:8

Psalm 147:5

Deuteronomy 32:4

Malachi 3:6

Psalm 103:13

Psalm 117:2

At the Fair: A Scary Moment

For months and months, Emily and her horse, Flash, had prepared for this day. Emily held on tightly to Flash's lead as they waited outside the fairgrounds arena. Soon it would be time to show off Flash and all the hard work they had done together to train for the halter competition at the county fair.

Emily quickly looked Flash over. Shiny coat . . . check! Clean hooves . . . check! Neatly combed mane and tail . . . check! Lead and halter secure . . . check!

Just as Emily finished her checklist, a voice announced over the microphone and loudspeaker: "Halter Class 1, proceed to the show-ring."

As Emily led Flash to line up with the other horses, he began to shake his head back and forth. Suddenly Flash reared up on his back legs.

"Oh, no!" thought Emily. "Something must have spooked Flash!"

Emily pulled on Flash's lead to try to direct him into place. "Please, Lord," Emily prayed, "help me keep Flash under control. Help me watch his hooves so he doesn't step on me or on anyone else. In Jesus' name I pray. Amen."

At the Fair: Answered Prayers

"Please, God," prayed Emily as she tried to get Flash under control. "Help me!"

After more pulling on the lead and words of frantic encouragement, Flash lowered his legs and calmed down. As Emily rubbed Flash on the nose, she silently prayed, "Thank You, God, for Your help."

When Flash was calm once more, another horse show entrant behind Emily called out, "Hey there, is everything okay?"

Emily turned around and saw the girl who called out to her. "Yes, I think my horse is calmed down now.

The girl behind Emily reached out her hand. "Hi, I'm Hannah."

As Emily reached out her hand, she noticed a blistered place on it where the lead had rubbed as she had tried to control Flash. Hannah saw it too.

"Oh, my!" said Hannah. "That must hurt."

"I didn't even notice it until now," replied Emily. "It's really sore. I'm not sure I'll be able to hold the lead to show Flash to the judges." A disappointed tear rolled down Emily's face.

Just then, Emily's mom and dad came to her side. Emily showed them her blistered hand.

"How am I going to be able to hold on to the lead and show Flash with this big sore?" Emily cried.

"Here's what we'll do," said Dad. "I'll stand here and take care of Flash while you and Mom go to the first-aid tent. It's right around the corner here from the arena. You have a little time because contestants are still lining up their horses to enter the ring.

Emily reluctantly handed Flash's lead over to her dad. "C'mon, Emily," her mom said. "We need to get moving so you can get back to the competition."

As Emily and her mom hurried out of the arena, Hannah called after them, "I'll pray for you, Emily. Hopefully the medics can bandage that hand and you'll be back right away."

Emily quickly glanced back at Hannah. "Thanks," she said.

At the Fair: In the Show-Ring

At the first-aid tent, the nurse examined Emily's blistered hand. She quickly cleaned the injured area, then spread soothing ointment on the blisters. Finally, she wrapped gauze around and around Emily's hand to protect it from further harm and to keep it clean.

Emily and her mom raced back to the arena. Flash and Emily's dad were still waiting to enter the show-ring.

"Whew!" exclaimed Emily. "We made it back in time!"

"How's your hand?" asked Dad.

"It feels better," said Emily. "At least I can hold on to Flash's lead now."

"That's great," said Dad. "Let's thank God for His healing help."

Emily and her mom and dad gathered together to pray. Emily's dad began, "Thank You, heavenly Father, for watching over Emily and for giving her the ability to calm down her horse. Thank You for providing medical help for Emily's injured hand. Help Emily now to be able to show Flash to the best of the abilities with which you've blessed her. We pray all these things in the name of Your Son, Jesus. Amen."

"Next into the ring, Contestant Number 10, Emily James, and her horse, Flash." The announcer's voice blared over the microphone and loudspeaker.

"Okay, Flash," Emily whispered to him as they began to walk toward the judge. "Let's show the judge some blue-ribbon stuff!"

Emily confidently led Flash in a walk to the judge in the show-ring. At the proper place in the ring, Emily led Flash to the left, and together they trotted around the ring so the judge could observe Flash's body and legs as he moved.

Now came the tough part. Under the direction of the ring steward, Emily was shown where she was to line up Flash alongside the other horses. Keeping a tight hold on Flash's lead, Emily placed Flash exactly where the steward directed. Quickly, with practiced movements, Emily maneuvered Flash's lead just the way they practiced to set up Flash's hind and front legs in the proper position for judging. Flash stood squarely in line with the other horses.

The judge came over and walked around Flash, closely observing his foot placement. After taking a few moments to mark down comments on his score sheet, the judge proclaimed, "Good job."

As the judge walked away to observe the next horse, Emily breathed a sigh of relief. She whispered in her horse's ear, "Yes, you *did* do a good job, Flash! No matter what, you are a blue-ribbon horse in my book!"

At the Fair: A Special Demonstration

"And the winner of the blue ribbon is . . . "

Emily's heart was beating fast as she awaited the judge's announcement.

"Contestant Number 10," the judge called.

"Way to go, Emily!" she heard her mom and dad call out from the arena stands.

The judge continued, "This is a bit unusual, I know, but before this group of contestants leaves the show-ring, I'd like Contestant Number 10 to demonstrate the excellent way she sets up her horse for judging. Contestant 10, please bring your horse to the center of the ring and face the other contestants," the judge instructed.

"Okay, Flash," Emily said to her prize-winning horse, "let's show everyone what we can do."

Emily led Flash to the center of the ring. Pulling gently on his lead, Emily used short tugs as she directed Flash to first plant his right hind leg, then move his left hind leg even with his right.

"Good horse, Flash," Emily praised.

With a few more short tugs, Flash adjusted his front feet so his body stood square. Each of Flash's legs were planted squarely under a corner of his body, neither too far apart nor too close together.

As Emily stood beside Flash, the judge pointed out to the other contestants the correct position of Flash's legs for showing.

"Once again, young lady, good job!" the judge told Emily. "Let's clear the ring now for the next class."

As Emily and Flash left the show-ring, her mom and dad ran up to her with big smiles.

"Great job, Emily!" her dad congratulated.

As she walked with her family, Emily silently prayed, "Thank You, God, for being with me and for helping me to do my best. Thank You for the opportunity to demonstrate to others what I've learned. In Jesus' name I pray. Amen."

At the Fair: Time with Dad

"Wow, Dad, the view of the fairgrounds from here is amazing!" marveled Emily as she and her father rode together on the Ferris wheel.

"It is, isn't it?" Emily's dad replied. "Being so high up also feels a whole lot cooler than it did in the horse show arena."

"That's for sure," said Emily. "It was really hot down in the show-ring."

"You did a great job today with Flash after a kind of scary beginning," Dad said proudly.

"Thanks, Dad. I didn't know how Flash would do for the judge after being spooked when we were lining up." Emily continued, "If not for your training, I wouldn't have known what to do. Thanks for all the time you spent with me showing how to work with Flash."

"You're welcome, dear daughter." Dad put his arm around Emily's shoulder as the Ferris wheel spun around. "That's one of the best parts of being a father. You get to teach your child fun things and get to spend time together. I love to talk to you and hear all about your hopes and plans. I'm especially pleased to see how your faith is growing. You show me how much you love and trust God when you pray to Him."

Emily smiled at her dad. "I love spending time with both my fathers: you *and* God, my Father *in heaven*!"

Emily pulled out her cell phone. "Hey, Dad, let's take a selfie to remember our time together today."

Emily snapped the photo, then showed it to her dad.

"I think Mom will love this," Emily beamed.

Just then, Emily's dad's cell phone vibrated. He turned to Emily and said, "Speaking of Mom . . . she just texted me!"

Emily's dad read his text.

"What did Mom want, Dad?" Emily asked.

"She says we all need to get over to the grandstand for the fair queen contest. The good seats are filling up fast!"

"Okay," said Emily as their car on the Ferris wheel slowed to a stop. As she and her dad exited the ride, Emily cried, "Let's go!"

At the Fair: Giving God Glory

At the grandstand, Emily and her dad saw Emily's mom waving at them from the front row of the bleachers. They quickly joined her.

"I'm glad you two made it," Emily's mom exclaimed. "The seats sure filled up fast."

"Look, Emily," said her dad. "I think the competition is about to begin."

As lively music played over the loudspeaker, the announcer of the pageant and five teenage contestants walked onto the stage in the center of the grandstand arena. The crowd applauded and cheered the name of their favorite contestant.

"Welcome to our fifty-first annual county fair queen pageant," the emcee began. "For the past fifty years, teenage girls from all over our county have competed for the title of county fair queen. With this title comes the honor of representing our county at parades, sporting events, business openings, and other occasions for the next twelve months. Tonight we have five young women hoping to be named fair queen. So let's begin."

For the next forty-five minutes, the pageant emcee interviewed each contestant. Based on the information they had submitted on their entry forms, the emcee asked them questions about their school activities, their families, their hobbies, and their plans for the future.

After their interviews, each girl performed a talent. Three played musical instruments. One juggled. The last contestant sang. The five young women then nervously took their seats and waited as the judges compiled the results.

"I wonder who will win," Emily whispered to her mom.

The emcee walked to the center of the stage. "Before we crown our new fair queen, I'd like to invite our outgoing fair queen, Miss Hannah Johnson, to say a few words."

The crowd cheered as Hannah walked up to the microphone. "Thank you, everyone, for the experience of serving as county fair queen this past year. I've had so much fun and have learned so many things about our county." Hannah paused for a moment, then looked up to the sky as she continued. "Most of all, I want to thank God and give Him all the glory for all the opportunities He has given me. God helped me every step of the way this year as I've served Him and you. Thank you, and may God bless all of you."

Hannah stepped to one side of the microphone as the emcee returned.

"The judges have made their decision," the emcee began. "Our fifty-first county fair queen is Miss Madison Anderson, sponsored by Quality Used Cars!"

Madison made her way to center stage. Hannah took off her crown and gently placed it on Madison's head.

"Put the Lord first in all you do," Hannah said to Madison, "and you'll have a wonderful year!"

At the Fair: An Invitation

After such an exciting first day at the county fair, Emily slept soundly. The next morning, she woke up with an idea.

"Hey, Mom and Dad," Emily called as she joined them in the kitchen for breakfast. "Today's armband day at the fair."

"Oh, that's right," said Dad. "Isn't that when you buy an armband for $20 and you can ride all the rides as many times as you want?"

"Yes," Emily replied, "and I was thinking . . ."

"Should we be worried?" teased Mom.

"No, I don't think so," Emily said. "But I was wondering if I could text Zoey to see if she could come with us. She doesn't get to go many places right now because her dad got laid off from his job. I've saved up some extra money from doing chores around the house. I've got enough to pay for Zoey's armband and for part of my own. I'm happy to do some extra chores to pay you back the rest."

"I think it's wonderful that you want to do something nice for Zoey," said Mom.

"So nice, in fact, that I think your mom and I can pay for both of your armbands," offered Dad.

"Really?" said Emily incredulously. "Mom and Dad, thanks so much! I'm going to text Zoey right now."

"Tell her we'll pick up at noon," Mom called out as Emily's fingers danced across her phone to text her friend.

By the time Emily, Zoey, and Emily's parents reached the fairgrounds, a big crowd had already gathered.

"Looks like there might be a record number of people here today," Emily's dad observed.

"Thanks so very much for inviting me and for paying my way," Zoey told Emily's parents.

"It's our pleasure!" Emily's mom replied. "Now, Emily," Mom continued, "Dad and I are going to look at some of the fair exhibits just over there, at the edge of the Midway. So we'll be close by, but I want you and Zoey to check in with us here by the Tilt-a-Whirl at 2:00 p.m." Emily's mom paused for a moment, then added, "You've got your cell phone, right?"

"Yes, Mom," said Emily, "and it's all charged up. We'll meet you back here at 2:00 sharp."

At the Fair: Staying Strong

The afternoon was quickly passing. Emily and Zoey had ridden every ride at least twice. After their third time on the Zipper, Zoey wiped her brow.

"Whew, it's really getting hot out here, don't you think, Emily?"

"I agree," said Emily as she looked up at the sky. "With all these clouds, you wouldn't think it would be so hot."

Just then, both girls heard a loud clap of thunder.

"Uh-oh," said Zoey. "I think it might storm."

Emily's cell phone rang. "It's my mom," she said as she tapped the screen to answer. "Hi, Mom. Did you hear that thunder?" Emily nodded her head. "Okay. Okay. Yes, I know where that is. Zoey and I will be right there."

Emily turned to Zoey. "Mom said there's a severe thunderstorm watch out for our county. She wants us to meet her and my dad at the entrance to the exhibit building right away. Mom said that's the safest place to wait out the storm."

"That's near the rides," Zoey replied. "But do you think we have time to get there before it starts raining?"

"If we hurry, I think we'll make it," said Emily. "Let's go!"

It seemed that all the people at the crowded fairgrounds had the same idea as Emily and Zoey. As fast as they tried to walk, it was impossible to move quickly among all the other fairgoers.

As Emily and Zoey inched their way toward the exhibit building, the sky grew darker and darker. The wind picked up. Drink cups and food wrappers whirled upward. Dust began to swirl. Lightning flashed everywhere.

"I'm scared, Emily," said Zoey.

"Me too," said Emily. She held out her hand to her friend. "Here. Grab my hand so we don't get separated in all these people. While we walk, let's pray that God will keep us safe."

"Okay," said Zoey.

"Heavenly Father," Emily began, "You control all things. Right now we are in danger from a big storm, and we need Your help. Please keep Zoey and me safe so that we can reach shelter. Thank You, Lord. Amen."

Torrents of rain suddenly began to fall from the sky. It was raining so hard it was difficult to see anything. Then the girls heard Emily's dad calling.

"Emily! Zoey! Move over to the right!" Dad called.

As the girls did so, Emily's dad appeared.

"Come on! Follow me! We're almost to the exhibit building."

Moments later, Emily, Zoey, and Emily's dad stepped into the safety of the exhibit building. Emily's mom saw them right away and rushed over to them with a dry sweatshirt and big bunch of paper towels.

"I'm so glad you're safe!" Emily's mom said as she hugged them all.

As the girls dried themselves off, they breathed a sigh of relief. "So are we! Thank You, God!"

At the Fair: God's Bountiful Blessings

"Whew!" said Zoey. "I'm glad we made it out of the rain."

"You and me both!" added Emily.

"Since it looks like it's going to rain for a while, why don't we look around here in the exhibition building at some of the things people have brought to display from their gardens," suggested Emily's mom.

"Good idea, dear," said Emily's dad.

"Hey, look at this here on the floor!" Emily called out as she walked among the tables of displayed garden vegetables.

"Wow!" exclaimed Zoey. "That's the biggest pumpkin I've ever seen! The tag says it weighs 826 pounds!"

"That pumpkin would make a lot of pumpkin pies," said Emily's dad. "Girls, did you know that 90–95 percent of all the processed pumpkin people eat in the United States comes from pumpkins grown in Illinois?"

"No, Dad, I didn't know that," said Emily. "Look at all these tomatoes. I didn't know that tomatoes could be yellow."

"Me neither," said Zoey. "The only ones I've ever seen are red. Look at this poster behind the tomato table. It says that Americans obtain more vitamins from tomatoes than any other vegetable."

"Since tomatoes are used to make ketchup, salsa, and spaghetti sauce and are used in all kinds of soups and stews, that makes sense," replied Emily's mom.

"These are some good-looking cucumbers in these pickle jars," Emily's dad said. "It says here that cucumbers are 96 percent water. I didn't know that."

"It also says that pickles originated in the country of India way back in ancient times. I always thought they came from a jar in the grocery store!" Zoey laughed.

"Mom and Dad, doesn't everything we have really come from God?" asked Emily.

"Absolutely!" said Emily's dad. "Foods like this are just one of the *many* blessings God gives us."

"Every day God blesses us with clothing, food, a place to live, good friends, good weather, good government, peace, and health," continued Emily's mom.

"Don't forget parents," said Emily.

"Or protection from things like dangerous storms," said Zoey. Zoey peered out the entrance of the exhibition hall. "Hey, it looks like the sun's coming out!"

"Great!" shouted Emily. "I'm ready for some more fair fun! C'mon, Zoey, let's go try out some of the games over by the carnival rides."

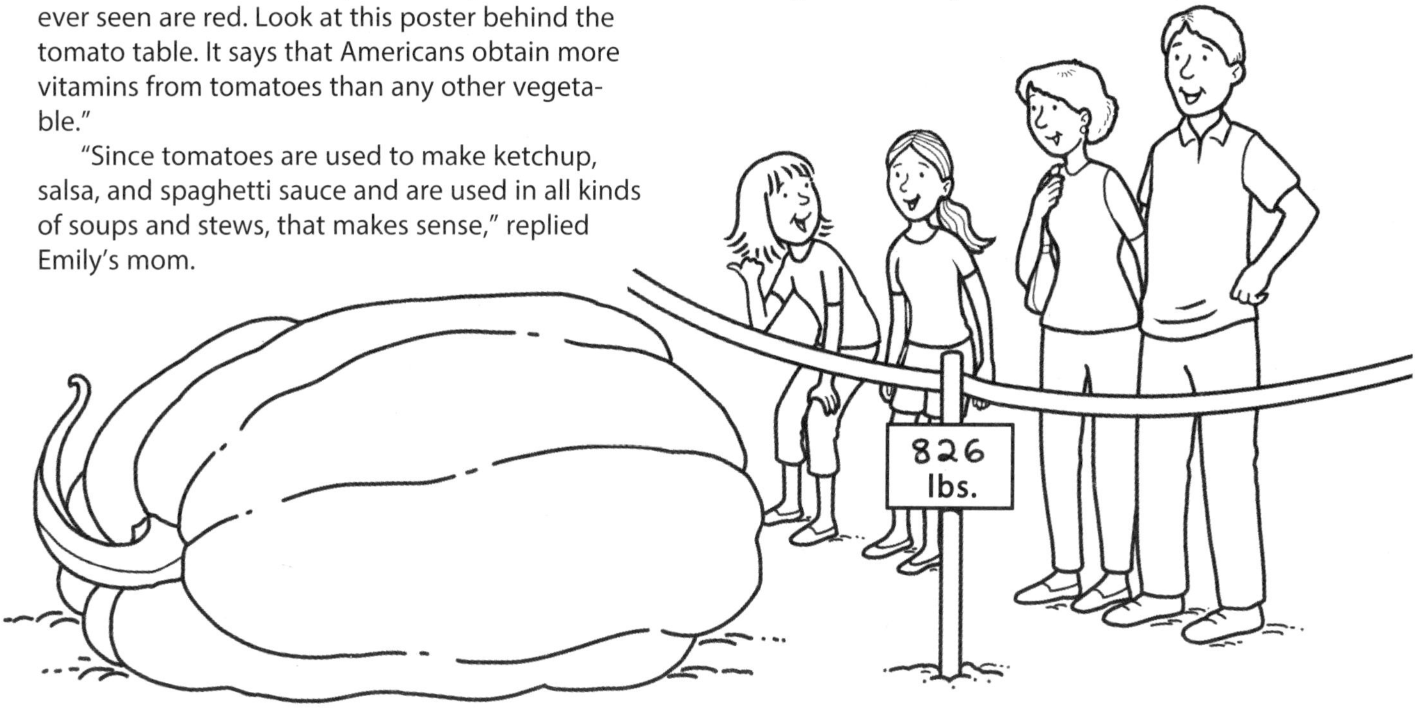

At the Fair: A Lesson in Forgiveness

"Girls," shouted Emily's mom as they sped off toward the carnival rides, "please be back here at the exhibition hall in an hour. And remember to stay together."

"Okay, Mom," Emily shouted. "C'mon, Zoey! I want to win a prize at the balloon dart game."

"Wait a minute," Zoey said as she stopped running. "Look over there." Zoey pointed to one of the livestock barns. "I see some lambs. Let's go take a look."

"I don't want to do that," Emily replied. "When you've seen one sheep, you've seen them all. The games are tons more fun. C'mon, Zoey."

"But we always do what you want to do," Zoey argued, her cheeks getting hot. "I don't feel like playing games right now. I'll probably lose my money and not win a prize. I want to look at the sheep."

"Well, if that's how you're going to be, fine with me," retorted Emily. "You can go look at your stupid sheep and I'll go win a prize at the carnival games. See you around." Emily stomped away.

Zoey watched her go. She thought, "Emily's mom said we should stay together. But I don't want to take a chance on those games. I want to go and see the sheep. I suppose we can meet up later at the exhibition hall." Zoey walked on to the sheep barn.

As Emily held out a dollar bill to the carnival worker to get some darts, a thought occurred to her. "Mom said that Zoey and I should stay together. I guess that's so we'll be safe here on the fairgrounds. Since Zoey's my guest here at the fair and my best friend, I guess I should have gone with her to see the sheep. This game can wait."

"I'm sorry," said Emily to the worker as she pulled back her hand. "I don't think I want to play this game right now."

Emily made her way back through the crowd and over to the sheep barn. She walked over to Zoey, who was gently petting one of the lambs on the head.

"Hi," Emily said shyly.

"Hi," Zoey sighed as she continued to pet the lamb.

Emily reached over the railing to pet the head of another lamb. "Wow! This lamb's wool is really soft!" Without even trying, a smile crept onto Emily's face. "They're so cute!"

Emily buried her fingers into two more sheeps' thick, woolly coats before she stopped to realize that she was actually having fun at the sheep barn. "I'm sorry," Emily admitted to Zoey. "I shouldn't have run off to do what I wanted. I should have gone with you to see the sheep."

"I forgive you, Emily," said Zoey. "And I'm sorry for wanting things my way and for getting angry with you. Maybe from now on we can take turns so we both get to see and do what we want here at the fair."

"Sounds like a great plan," said Emily, with her biggest smile of the afternoon.

At the Fair: Tempted Tummies

As Emily and Zoey walked away from the lambs at the sheep barn, Emily looked at her watch. "We better start walking back to the exhibition hall. Our hour is almost up."

As the girls walked past the food booths, they were bombarded with delicious smells.

"Wow!" exclaimed Zoey. "This part of the fair sure smells better than the animal barns." Zoey pointed to a nearby food truck. "Oh boy, funnel cakes! They're my favorite!" Zoey reached into her pocket and pulled out a ten-dollar bill. "My dad gave me this money. He said I should use it to treat us both to something good to eat at the fair. Would you like a funnel cake and a soda?"

Emily glanced at her watch again. "I don't know, Zoey. I think we'll probably eat dinner once we get back to my mom and dad. Maybe we should wait until after supper."

"You're probably right," Zoey sighed. "But they sure do smell good," she added longingly.

Emily saw the disappointed look on Zoey's face. "Well, they probably won't make us too full," Emily reasoned. "Let's go for it! But don't tell my mom we ate a snack so close to supper."

Zoey purchased a funnel cake and a large soda for herself and the same for Emily. Eagerly, the girls devoured the treats on their way back to the exhibition hall.

Emily was right about her mom and dad wanting to get some dinner. As soon as the girls met them, they all went back to the food vendors.

"Here's a booth with some barbecued pork sandwiches," Emily's mom announced. "I think these would taste good right about now. Don't you agree, girls?"

Emily and Zoey quickly glanced at each other. "Sure," said Zoey quietly.

"I'm in," added Emily halfheartedly.

Emily and Zoey dutifully ate a sandwich each, along with some waffle fries and another soda. By the last few bites, the girls could hardly swallow their food.

"You two seem awfully full for just eating a sandwich and a few fries," Emily's dad observed.

"I guess if you're both hungry later, you can get a snack after the tractor pull competition," said Emily's mom.

The girls walked slowly to the grandstand behind Emily's parents. As they climbed the bleachers to their seats, both girls rubbed their stomachs. As the tractors warmed up their engines, the powerful vibration made the bleachers shake. Emily and Zoey both felt a little sick to their stomachs. As the diesel smoke from the tractors' smoke stacks wafted over the grandstand, each girl put her hands over her nose and mouth as their nausea got worse.

Emily's mom looked over at the two sick friends. Above the noise of the roaring engines, she shouted, "What's wrong, girls?"

"Mom," Emily confessed, "Zoey and I each ate a funnel cake and had a soda right before we ate dinner. Now our stomachs really hurt."

Emily's mom reached into her purse and pulled out two peppermint candies.

"A little peppermint soothes sick stomachs," she said as she gave one to each girl.

Emily and Zoey let the candies slowly dissolve in their mouths, and in a short time both girls felt much better.

"I think you've both learned what eating too much fair food can do," Emily's mom said.

"Sorry, Mom," Emily said. "The smell of the funnel cakes was so tempting, Zoey and I just couldn't resist."

"I guess you girls were pulled right to that funnel cake booth like those tractors are pulling those heavy sleds down the track," laughed Emily's dad.

"Not funny, Dad," groaned Emily.

At the Fair: Delivered from Danger

As the tractor pull ended, the announcer's voice came over the loudspeaker.

"Ladies and gentlemen, boys and girls, don't get out of your seats just yet. Tonight we have an exciting surprise for you! We are privileged to have with us motorcycle daredevil Flaming Frank Fitzgerald! Flaming Frank is famous for jumping his motorcycle through flaming hoops of fire. Tonight he is attempting to set his personal best record by jumping his motorcycle through five flaming hoops at once! Friends, you don't want to miss this!"

"Ooh!" exclaimed Emily. "This sounds exciting!"

"I think it sounds dangerous," said Emily's mom.

"I wonder if he'll do it," added Zoey.

Flaming Frank's road crew quickly set up the motorcycle ramp and the five hoops. When everything was ready, Flaming Frank rode into the grandstand arena to the applause of the crowd.

"Ladies and gentlemen," the announcer called. "For this extremely dangerous trick, Flaming Frank is wearing a special flame-retardant jumpsuit regulated to protect him in temperatures up to a thousand degrees."

"That's pretty hot," remarked Emily's dad.

The announcer continued, "Flaming Frank also wears a specially-designed helmet and face mask not only to protect him from the burning flames but also to help cushion his head, should he crash. Heavy gloves and flame-retardant boots complete Flaming Frank's protective costume. Are you ready, Flaming Frank?"

Flaming Frank bowed his head for a moment.

"He's praying," said Emily.

Then Frank lifted his head and gave a thumbs-up as he revved the engine of his motorcycle.

"Okay, crew," the announcer shouted. "It's time to light the hoops!"

Flaming Frank's crew ran into action. One by one, they used their flaming torches to light the fuel-drenched hoops.

As the crew extinguished the torches, the announcer called, "Okay, crowd. After I say 'One, Two, Three,' you yell 'Go!' Ready? One! Two! Three!"

"GO!" yelled the audience.

Flaming Frank sped up the motorcycle ramp. Emily, Zoey, and the rest of the crowd shouted as he flew through the furiously flaming hoops, "One! Two! Three! Four! Five! Oh, no!"

As Flaming Frank roared through the fifth hoop, the back tire of his motorcycle caught the left side of the burning hoop. Not only did the hoop fly sideways through the air, but so did Flaming Frank and his motorcycle. Frank and his bike ended up on their sides, about fifty feet from the end of the ramp. The flaming hoop rolled toward one corner of the arena, where it continued to burn.

The crowd was completely quiet. Flaming Frank's crew sprang into action again. They ran to Frank, brandishing fire extinguishers and a first-aid kit. From under the grandstand, an ambulance siren wailed as the vehicle sped near the area where Frank lay still.

"Is Flaming Frank okay?" Zoey whispered to Emily.

"I don't know. He fell pretty hard."

After what seemed like forever, the paramedics and Frank's crew stepped away from him. Slowly Frank stood, took off his helmet, and waved triumphantly to the crowd.

As the audience cheered their relief, a local news reporter ran up to Flaming Frank, microphone in hand.

"Flaming Frank," the reporter began, "any thoughts on your fabulously flaming jump?"

"Just one," said Frank as he looked upward. "Thank You, God, for Your protection and deliverance."